FOOTBALL'S FEARLESS ACTIVISTS

FOOTBALL'S FEARLESS ACTIVISTS

HOW COLIN KAEPERNICK, ERIC REID, KENNY STILLS, AND FELLOW ATHLETES STOOD UP TO THE NFL AND PRESIDENT TRUMP

MIKE FREEMAN

SPORTS
PUBLISHING

Sports Publishing books may be purchased in bulk at special discounts for sales promotion, corporate gifts, fund-raising, or educational purposes. Special editions can also be created to specifications. For details, contact the Special Sales Department, Sports Publishing, 307 West 36th Street, 11th Floor, New York, NY 10018 or sportspubbooks@skyhorsepublishing.com.

Sports Publishing® is a registered trademark of Skyhorse Publishing, Inc.®, a Delaware corporation.

Visit our website at www.sportspubbooks.com.

10 9 8 7 6 5 4 3 2 1

Library of Congress Cataloging-in-Publication Data is available on file.

Jacket design by Brian Peterson
Cover photo credit: Getty Images

Print ISBN: 978-1-68358-350-9
Ebook ISBN: 978-1-68358-351-6

Printed in the United States of America

To Ella, the best daughter in the universe.
The future is bright because you will help change the world.

CONTENTS

CONTENTS

Preface

TOLL

There are many heroes in this story. Some of the names, like Colin Kaepernick and Eric Reid, you may know. There are others you may not. One of those is Kenny Stills. Of all the heroes in this inspiring, sad, tumultuous tale, he is one of the most unique.

When Kaepernick began protesting in 2016, changing the sports world and attracting the attention of US presidents, world leaders, civil rights activists, NFL leadership, and white nationalists, Stills seemed like an unlikely candidate to join Kaepernick and other NFL players taking a knee. He grew up near a military base in San Diego, California, a staunch military town. His mentor, like a father to Stills, was a marine for over twenty years. The protests were often portrayed by right-wing media as anti-cop and anti-military. This was far from the truth, yet the narrative was set.

"I don't think you should do this," the former marine told him. "They seem like they're against the military."

"They're not," Stills told him. "They just want change. They just want the police to stop killing us."

"I felt that if I did nothing," Stills says now, "I wouldn't be able to live with myself. I didn't want to look back at my life and say, 'You could have done something. But you didn't. You were a coward.'"

Stills prepared for what he knew would be an arduous trip, from a relatively unknown wide receiver for the Miami Dolphins to a well-known and revered freedom fighter to some, and ungrateful anti-cop, anti-military, anti-American troublemaker to others. Like other NFL players, like Kaepernick, he didn't care. The league needed player voices to counter what was a plague of police violence against people of color, and he was going to be part of the chorus—even if it cost him.

Stills began reading extensively about the civil rights movement and any lessons that could be gleamed and utilized for this fight. He listened to Malcolm X's biography on audiobook. He traveled to various places in the South that were epicenters of the fights for civil rights in the 1960s. He went to the Lorraine Motel where Martin Luther King Jr. was killed. He walked across the Edmund Pettus Bridge in Selma, Alabama, where protesters were assaulted by police. He read the biography of Congressman John Lewis, one of the men attacked that day in Selma.

Stills looked inward too. In a mini documentary he made in 2018 titled *Kenny Stills*, he spoke of the impact police brutality, and to a larger degree racism, had on people of color: "I don't think people really understand what it's like to look in the mirror and feel like you're not important, nobody gives a shit," said Stills. "If you didn't play football, you're irrelevant, because of your skin tone. I didn't choose this [skin]. I was born [like] this. This is me. Did I do something wrong? Or I was just born, so I'm wrong?"

He also listened to the opinions of not just teammates and friends but family as well. All while continuing to work with kids, at the time, in the Miami community. No Dolphins player had donated more time working with the community than Stills. It was a normal scene for Stills to leave practice and drive directly to a charity or community event.

It's in this space, and in this time, where heroes are birthed, though not always recognized, and where sacrifices are made, though not always seen. Kaepernick and Reid's bravery were the ignition source, but a handful of players—maybe five to seven total out of the approximately 1,700 active NFL players—kept protesting for several years after Kaepernick first took a knee to protest an unjust criminal justice system and the shootings of unarmed people of color by the police. Stills was one of those players.

He refused to lose his sense of independence and wanted to do what he believed was right, even after it was revealed that Miami Dolphins owner Stephen Ross, a Donald Trump supporter, once hosted a fundraiser for Trump's campaign. Not long after the protests began, the NFL invested almost $90 million into a newly formed social justice partnership called the Players Coalition. Kaepernick, Reid, Stills, and several other players left the Coalition not long after its creation believing the money—a pittance to billionaire NFL owners—was being used to buy off players and stop them from protesting. The original $90 million was divided by all 32 franchises, or about $2.8 million a team. The NFL is a private entity, so knowing exactly how much the NFL makes in totality is impossible. *Bloomberg* estimated its profits, mainly from television revenue, were $13 billion in 2016, $14 billion in 2017, and $15 billion in 2018. Commissioner Roger Goodell has targeted $25 billion in revenue by 2027.

Part of Stills's story, as well as that of a handful of other players, is the impact protesting had on their physical and mental health. Kaepernick, of course, after the 49ers, was unable to get another job. As of late 2020, he remains unsigned. Other players suffered in different ways. One player who protested briefly said the ensuing death threats—several dozen over a three-month period in 2018—caused him to contemplate suicide.

Some players lost lifelong friends. There were teammates who stopped speaking to them. Relationships with loved ones suffered.

This was just part of the toll that some protesting players, who took a knee or raised a fist, endured for years while we all watched from afar, having no clue they were paying this price.

Stills said once he began protesting, he began receiving racist and threatening notes and horrific messages on social media. "People told me to kill myself," Stills explained. "To hang myself."

At one point, during a game at Carolina, a persistent heckler kept verbally attacking Stills all game. "Carolina was awful," Stills told Natalie Weiner of *Bleacher Report*. "This guy was pretty liquored up in the front row right behind the bench. Sometimes it's pretty sad, honestly—the fact that people really don't understand and they're not trying to understand. It kind of breaks your heart."

Brandon Marshall, a linebacker with the Denver Broncos, also protested. He was sent a letter that contained a violent threat, and others that were full of racial slurs. One person came to the team facility and burned one of his jerseys. As he told the website

Complex, which detailed everything that happened to Marshall, he also lost two endorsements.

Stills in another instance, on social media, was told by one person to "go jump off a bridge, you ungrateful nigger."

* * *

"At the beginning," Stills said, "it was pretty nerve-racking. Not going to lie, it was at times terrifying."

Why?

"You knew you could lose everything," Stills said. "You could lose your job. There were some guys who worried they could lose more than that."

Some players were concerned that an extremist might sneak a gun into a stadium and kill protesting players as they took a knee.

In other cases, players were simply worried about their safety and the well-being of their children. In 2017, Dolphins safety Michael Thomas stood before cameras when explaining why he was protesting, and when speaking about the future of his daughter, began crying. "It was the craziest thing—emotions were already running high because of the Trump comments, and we'd lost, so I was pissed," Thomas told Weiner. "But once I got to talking about my daughter, I couldn't even control it. After that, people who didn't necessarily agree with the protest hit me up because they saw a father trying to be protective of his daughter and her future. People changed their tone, because it became real to them."

For Stills, the moment that changed everything for him was the summer of 2016 when a spate of unarmed men of color were killed by police. On consecutive days in July, Alton Sterling and

Philando Castile were killed. Two months later, Terence Crutcher was killed, only five days after Stills began protesting. No police officer was ever charged in the Sterling killing, and the police officers involved in the other two killings were acquitted by juries.

"I looked at friends and family, who looked like me," Stills said, "and I thought that to some police, and to the court system, my life doesn't matter. The color of my skin to some people means I'm inferior and don't deserve certain rights. I wanted to fight this, and while I understood what could happen to my career, I didn't care. I wanted to make change, and this was the way to do it."

The toll was known, but Stills was going to pay it no matter the cost.

After a public spat with Ross, he was traded on August 31, 2019—along with former first-round pick Laremy Tunsil, a fourth-round pick (2020), and a sixth-round pick (2021)—to the Houston Texans for two first-round picks (2020 and 2021), a second-round pick (2021), Johnson Bademosi, and Julie'n Davenport. Those are all just names and datapoints, and they don't address what his trade actually meant. No, Stills wasn't effectively banned from the NFL, like Kaepernick, but he had to leave Miami, a place he loved. He was like the other players who took a knee. All of the owners should have cherished him, but instead, many of them feared him.

In Houston, he became a valuable part of one of the best offenses in the game. More important, he is one of the most respected men inside the Texans' locker room. Off the field, as he did in Miami, he works extensively with kids and also helps to bridge the gap between African Americans and the police by helping to keep lines of communication open between the two entities. He began part-nering with the Houston Police Department almost immediately after arriving in the city.

"He's not out to condemn the police, he's not out to condemn good policing," Houston Police Chief Art Acevedo told the *Houston Chronicle*. "He's out to lift good policing, lift up good police officers, help bridge any gap between the community, and especially young people, but he also wants to make sure we have a culture of accountability."

One of the most important things Stills and the protesters did was force the nation to reexamine its relationship with the military and law enforcement. Many Americans are comfortable with that deference. The protesting players showed many others were not and agreed that the relationship needed further examination. Award-winning documentarian Ken Burns told author Howard Bryant in the book *The Heritage: Black Athletes, a Divided America, and the Politics of Patriotism* the difference between our views now about war and the military and, say, the Vietnam Era, is the draft. The draft allows the country to (mostly) share some of the responsibilities of fighting wars (unless your rich daddy can say you have bone spurs and buy your way out of the war). Now, the volunteer Army has created a small and separate military class that many people never see or experience. This leads to a built-in reverence, since military members are doing things most Americans aren't willing to. (I remember flying home from Army basic training and people stopping me in the airport to thank me for my service and I thought, *Why are you thanking me? I volunteered to do this shit!*)

I wasn't a super soldier. I wasn't in special forces. I was just a grunt, joining out of high school out of a sense of duty and patriotism, serving initially on active duty, and then in the National Guard. I didn't need the money for college; I grew up solidly middle class. I just thought this is what Americans should do, and I wasn't alone. I met many other soldiers who felt the same way.

That anyone would say Stills was anti-military was remarkably offensive to me. I joined to protect everything America stood for, and one of the biggest things it represents is freedom of speech. Beyond that, the protests were never anti-military nor anti-police. Not once did I think he's disrespecting me or the men and women I served with.

The protests were extremely personal for me in another way that went beyond my military service. In March 2012, my best friend was shot and killed by a New Jersey state trooper on the side of the highway. The officer said my friend attacked him with a flashlight. He shot him three times.

I will never believe that my friend attacked a police officer. Or, hell, anyone. I'm like a number of African Americans who lost a friend or loved one to a police shooting and don't believe the version given by the cops. I will always believe my friend was unjustly killed.

Before I headed to basic training in Oklahoma, my friend came to my house, punched me, and said, "Good luck, bro. Love you, and we'll party when you get back."

* * *

In February 2020, a teacher at a Houston-area high school reached out to Stills to have him speak to their class during Black History

Month. Stills not only responded, he FaceTime'd with the class. The teacher thanked Stills on Twitter:

> "I want to give Kenny Stills a huge shout out. . . . I reached out to him a couple of weeks ago. . . . We started our Civil Rights unit this morning and I always use NFL players kneeling as a current example ever since the movement started. Well he took time out of his vacation to audio record some questions I sent him pertaining to our unit and then FaceTime'd my class encouraging them to be the change they want to see. . . . Words cannot express how thankful I am to . . . Kenny Stills for setting this up and doing this for my students. He could've politely declined but he knew how important this history is and that there's still change that needs to be made."

Throughout the 2020 season, there were, by the author's count, just four kneelers. Three were players, and then Kayla Morris, a cheerleader for the San Francisco 49ers, bravely kneeled for most of the movement.

Now is the time to chronicle what happened, and now is the time to look at the players who fueled it, like Stills.

Stills is the best of what the NFL has to offer. In many ways, he is the best of what human beings have to offer.

He is, most of all, one of the heroes.

Introduction

THREAT ASSESSMENT

One thing we know for certain, all these years later, is that Colin Kaepernick was right.

When he spoke of the crisis that was police brutality against black and brown people . . . he was right. When he took a knee in protest because he knew, like others, just how awful things really were for people of color in the judicial system . . . he was right. When he'd name the victims, like Alton Sterling, and some Americans didn't care they were dead because they were black men . . . he was right. When Ahmaud Arbery was gunned down by two white men while jogging in Brunswick, Georgia, in February 2020, and news of the horrific event erupted across the country, several NFL players started texting each other about the incident, remembering the protests, and one player said he thought . . . *yeah, Colin was right.* When a Minneapolis police officer was recorded putting his knee on the neck of George Floyd, who uttered multiple times he couldn't breathe, and then later died, you couldn't help but think . . . he was right.

Most of all, Colin Kaepernick lost everything because . . . he was right.

Now, you may say, "Of course he was right," but large swaths of the country didn't believe him. They thought he was selfish, unpatriotic, and a cop-hater. They thought the notion that people of color being killed by police was because, well, if only they had followed the cop's orders, they would still be alive. Everything crystalized in the fall of 2016. It was a short time after Kaepernick's protest had started, and one that had morphed into a rare NFL story that jumped out of the football ecosystem and into the mainstream. Kaepernick and fellow San Francisco 49ers teammate Eric Reid were unrelenting in their stance. They were called brave and smart by some, while others called them anti-police and claimed they hated the military. None of that mattered to Kaepernick. To him, this moment was a matter of life and death for Americans of color, and nothing was going to prevent him from bringing attention to the issue.

"People were telling him to stop," remembers Reid. "People were threatening him. They were saying they were going to kill him. Kill his family. The NFL wanted him to stop. He was feeling pressure from everywhere. But he is one of the strongest people I've ever known. He wasn't going to stop."

Teammates could tell the story was shifting from one that sparked curiosity and outrage into something different, something more potent that could mushroom into something larger. At the time, no one knew what that thing could be, but it was morphing into a different shape. Everyone on the 49ers knew it—even the younger players.

Being a rookie in the NFL is like walking in a fierce storm. The footing is loose, and teams purposefully throw everything at them to see if they crumble. And off the field, many rookies try to keep an extremely low profile. Making news in the wrong way can lead to fines or even getting cut by the team. That's why what happened next was so remarkable.

A few weeks after Kaepernick's protest began, while standing at his locker, a group of offensive and defensive rookies approached him with an unusual request. They wanted to join Kaepernick and Reid's protests.

It was a fiercely supportive gesture, and while Kaepernick was appreciative, he knew he couldn't accept it. He knew, without question, that if the rookies joined him, it would negatively impact their careers. If they protested, they could actually end them before they'd begun.

"Focus on your careers," Kaepernick told them. "I love you guys, but I don't want you to do this."

This remains perhaps the least discussed, yet most important, aspect of Kaepernick's protest. He knew that by protesting there was a good chance—if not a total lock—that it would lead to him never playing in the NFL again. He didn't want anyone else to suffer that same potential fate.

There are many different types of sacrifices. There are soldiers who lose their lives protecting their country. One of those people was former Arizona Cardinals safety Pat Tillman, who soon after the September 11 attacks quit the NFL to join the Army Rangers. The Army initially lied about how Tillman died while fighting in Afghanistan but eventually admitted it was due to friendly fire.

Several years before that, when I was interviewing Tillman, he once told me how NFL players needed to use their power and visibility more "for the benefit of working class people, and I mean working class people of all races." He looked at me. "You could do more too."

"Me?"

"Yeah, you," he said.

"You're a white guy, telling a black guy he needs to do more for poor people," I responded.

"I do my part," he said. "What do you do?"

"I walk around as a black guy," I said.

There are only a handful of athletes who consistently backed up their words with actions. The NFL protesters were some of those people. Tillman obviously was as well. He backed up his words about sacrifice by giving his life to defend his country.

There are other types of sacrifices, however. There are single parents who are selfless in raising their children. Or Jim Crow era civil rights leaders who were murdered fighting for the rights of African Americans. Or football players who sacrifice their bodies catching a pass across the middle of the field. Sacrifices come in many different shapes and sizes. Kaepernick didn't give up his life, but in an act of selflessness, he knew, he definitely knew, he was sacrificing his career. There are few people who would do that—for anything.

"I think what's sometimes forgotten, or ignored, about Colin, is that he's someone with high character," says defensive lineman Martellus Bennett. "It was never a shock that Colin did what he did by starting the protests because, to me, that's what someone of high character does."

* * *

If you want to truly begin to understand why the NFL reacted with such fury, and fear, to Colin Kaepernick's protest movement and later targeted that anger toward Kaepernick alone, the answer partly begins here, in this book, with three moments of honesty. The first one is from an NFL owner, who had a conversation with me and requested to remain anonymous:

> There were one or two owners who liked what Colin was doing. They thought his cause was honorable. Most of the other owners were terrified of him. The way some of them spoke about him, it was like they were doing threat assessments. [The owner was asked to clarify.]
>
> Some owners think of things in terms of solely, or mostly, about their money. What threatens their income? Will a new tax code lessen how much money they will take in? Will a domestic violence case cause fans to tune out? They looked at Colin and the protests, some owners did, as a threat to their revenue model. That's what I mean by threat assessment. Then add to all of that Donald Trump was trashing us, some owners genuinely believed the whole thing could come crashing down.

"You mean some owners believed the protest movement was a threat to the NFL's existence?" I asked.

> Yes, some owners believed that. Yes, that's accurate. Not that they thought there'd be no NFL but that the revenue would crash and the Fox News of the world, and Trump, could cause mass boycotts. That was always greatly exaggerated, but that was the fear.
>
> There were also owners that just hated him. Race played a part in that. The inherent belief some hold that cops can do no wrong was also part of it. When things really got hot, and the whole country was talking about this, I had an owner tell me, "If

the blacks just listen to cops, they won't get shot." Yes, he said, "the blacks." Keep in mind the league is about 65 percent African American. So that's what you're dealing with. Not to mention most of the owners, by far, are Trump supporters.

The other concern was Colin's movement would spread to every locker room. The thought was that Colin would cause large number of players to really examine how business was done in the NFL. Some owners thought Colin would get players to push for more rights, like guaranteed salaries. One owner said, "He'll get them to strike."

When I look back at the time, what I mainly see is fear. Owners were afraid of Colin, and there was no reason to be.

When asked why he didn't publicly back Kaepernick if he agreed with the protests, the owner said, "Because I was scared too."

* * *

Now, here's a moment of honesty from an NFL general manager, who also requested to remain anonymous:

When Colin was a free agent, I took a hard look at him and thought about signing him. I watched a lot of his tape, and the year the 49ers went to the Super Bowl [XLVII in 2012 season] he was brilliant. I thought hard about signing him or, at least, talking to him. But I knew what the answer from our owner would be. I asked my [assistant general manager], and he confirmed what I thought. I remember his face when I brought up the idea of signing Colin, and he looked at me like, "Are you fucking crazy? He'll [the owner] never let you do it." So I dropped the whole thing. I suspect that's how conversations went inside a number of different buildings.

He could have really helped us. He could have helped a lot of teams, but no one wanted to touch him. When I asked other GMs and personnel guys about him, the response was usually similar. I had one guy tell me, "If I go to my owner about signing Colin, he'll burn my house down."

I don't believe there was an official edict from owners, or the league office, saying not to sign him. I think a lot of general managers just understood it wasn't going to happen. No one wants to rock the boat. If you do, if you're not viewed as a team player, you'll be ostracized. An owner might think you're not worth the trouble. Your ass will get fired, and you'll never work in the league again.

* * *

Finally, here's a moment of honesty from an NFL head coach:

I never believed that Kaepernick was a great player. I thought he was okay. Not bad. Not great. Okay.

None of that changes how I thought what happened to him was one of the worst things I've seen in all my years [over two decades] of coaching football. We should all be ashamed of ourselves, as a league, including me for not speaking up. He was more than good enough to be in the NFL and be a starter. He's not my kind of player, but he's a player in this league. To pretend otherwise is just a lie.

He was better than at least 25 percent of the starting quarterbacks in the NFL. That's a low estimate.

I asked, "Why didn't more coaches push to sign Kaepernick if he was that much better?"

"Coaches hate distractions."

"What about when teams sign players who commit crimes like sexual assault or are drug users?"

To most coaches, those aren't distractions. Those things are a part of football. I think from top of the league on down to the coaches, we were all afraid. We were afraid of protests. We were afraid of Trump. We were afraid of losing money or our jobs. You hear people in the NFL talk about principles and family. I'm not a Colin fan, but we betrayed everything we say we stand for.

* * *

The main story of the protests is about the opposite of fear. It's about the fearlessness of these men who ignited a movement and stood up to the most powerful league in the history of American sports; a Fox News empire, which combined with other conservative media to become dedicated to destroying them; and a POTUS using them as a racial wedge.

"I don't think that people understand how much some black players were worried about Trump all along," says Kenny Stills. "I saw some of the things he said as a candidate, like Mexicans are rapists, and I was really worried. When he became president and continued to say other ugly things, and not just about us as players, a lot of players started talking about how he wasn't just a danger to all people of color, but he was threat to our entire country and democracy. Even now, there are white players who supported him, who've stopped because they don't trust him either."

All significant movements start with this kind of foresight but also with raw fearlessness, and Kaepernick's was no different. Yet what makes this situation so unique in sports history is how a twenty-nine-year-old didn't just fight the NFL or the entirety of the American judicial system, he took on a president. Never before in this country's history has a president attacked a sports figure. Not Jackie Robinson, who broke the color barrier. Not Cleveland Browns running back Jim Brown, who spoke frequently and passionately about the evils of racism. Not Tommie Smith or John Carlos, who famously raised black-gloved fists during the 1968 Summer Olympics. No one. Kaepernick was the first sports civil rights leader who had a president trying to destroy him.

In an article that appeared in *The Nation*—a progressive magazine and website that covers politics and culture—former *New York Times* journalist Robert Lipsyte wrote on this notion in a July 2018 story called "Donald Trump's War on Black Athletes":

> Snatching immigrant babies may have scored some points for President Trump with his base, but it was never going to light up the scoreboard like tackling black jocks. That one really played to the grandstands. The complicated combination of adoration and resentment so many white males feel for those rich, accomplished über-men is a significant but rarely discussed aspect of fandom, especially in relation to football, that *magna cum macho* of American sports. . . . When the commander in chief of toxic masculinity dubbed any football player who didn't stand during the playing of the national anthem a "son of a bitch," the war on black men took a spectacular pop-cultural surge. And unlike white cops who shoot unarmed black men, President Trump didn't even have to claim that he had been afraid.

"For white players it's about the fear of losing their jobs," David Meggyesy, a white former NFL linebacker who, in the 1960s, set a standard for racial outspokenness, told Lipsyte. "But too many white fans share Trump's tribalism that includes seeing white players as the brains and black players as the bodies, not too smart, who should just 'shut up and play.'

"Trump, once a pro football owner himself, clearly understands a white male mindset in which black football players exist only to provide on-field thrills, never to be humanized, much less allowed to protest inequality and racism.[1] Meanwhile, the players, most of whom know that they are easily replaceable, often lacking guaranteed contracts, exist at the sufferance of their white billionaire team owners, a number of whom were early Trump donors."

It would be a mistake, however, to think this was only about race relations between blacks and whites. African American athletes were simply convenient targets. Since announcing his run for office, Trump has pushed to ban Muslims from entering the country and trafficked in ugly stereotypes of Jewish people. He infamously kicked off his campaign by casting Mexicans as rapists and killers. "When Mexico sends its people, they're not sending their best," he said. "They're not sending you. They're not sending you. They're sending people that have lots of problems, and they're bringing those problems with us. They're bringing drugs. They're bringing crime. They're rapists. And some, I assume, are good people."

Two *New York Times* reporters, Julie Hirschfeld Davis and Michael D. Shear, described a meeting Trump was holding with some staff about a border wall in their book on the Trump administration *Border Wars: Inside Trump's Assault on Immigration*. "Privately, the president had often talked about fortifying a border wall with a water-filled trench, stocked with snakes or alligators, prompting aides to seek a cost estimate," the book states. "He wanted the wall electrified, with spikes on top that could pierce human flesh. After publicly suggesting that soldiers shoot migrants if they threw rocks, the president backed off when his staff told him that was illegal.

---

1   Trump owned the USFL's New Jersey Generals, from 1984 to 1985.

But later in a meeting, aides recalled, he suggested that they shoot migrants in the legs to slow them down. That's not allowed either, they told him."

In January 2018, as the *Washington Post* wrote:

Trump grew frustrated with lawmakers who came to the Oval Office to finds a way to protect immigrants from developing nations with large black populations.

"Why are we having all these people from shithole countries come here?" the president asked, according to those in the meeting.

"Why do we need more Haitians?" Trump added. "Take them out."

And days before the 2018 midterm election, the president characterized individuals crossing the border and seeking asylum as violent criminals terrorizing law enforcement and others on their way to wreak havoc in the United States.

"Some people call it an 'invasion,'" he said. "It's like an invasion. They have violently overrun the Mexican border.

"They've overrun the Mexican police, and they've overrun and hurt badly Mexican soldiers," Trump added. "So this isn't an innocent group of people. It's a large number of people that are tough. They've injured, they've attacked, and the Mexican police and military has actually suffered."

Trump called California "a disgrace to our country"; said that Chicago was "embarrassing to us as a nation"; called Baltimore "a disgusting, rat and rodent infested mess"; and said four congresswomen of color should "go back" to the countries they came from . . . even though one of the women was from Detroit, another was born in Cincinnati, and a third was born in the Bronx.

No, the Trump era isn't solely about white versus black. It's about white—or Trump's version of it—versus almost every other race and religious belief, or part of the country that doesn't fit what he thinks of as American.

All of this is the core story of football's fearless fighters. Its roots aren't recent or shallow. This an old problem of race and class that goes back to the origins of this nation, which started with the beginning of the near eradication of Native Americans.

It's also a story of hope, love, and kindness at a time when fear and division took hold during one of the ugliest periods in recent American history. It's also a story of sacrifice. It is, as Kaepernick once told me when I stood next to him at his locker in San Francisco, about a simple thing: refusing to stop doing what you believe is right, even if you know it might cost you everything.

"I don't care if this makes me unpopular," Kaepernick said, just a short time after his protest began. "I'm going to fight for black and brown lives. Because we are dying and this has to stop. I'm going to keep fighting as long as it takes. I don't care if it takes the rest of my life."

Chapter 1

AMOK TIME

"Darkness cannot drive out darkness: only light can do that.
Hate cannot drive out hate; only love can do that."

—Dr. Martin Luther King Jr.

President Donald Trump was holding a rally on a warm Monday night in Louisville, Kentucky. It was March 2017. He pulled a sheet of paper out of his jacket suit and before reading what was on it almost started chuckling. He began talking about "the San Francisco quarterback."

"There was an article today," Trump explained. "It was reported that NFL owners don't want to pick him up because they don't want to get a nasty tweet from Donald Trump. Do you believe that? I just saw that. I just saw that. I said if I remember that one I'm gonna report it to the people of the Kentucky. Because they like it when people actually stand for the American flag."

No politician relishes confrontation more than Trump. It's attempting to ban Muslims (even those who were legal citizens). Or spending years saying the first black president wasn't born in

1

America. Or publicly calling for the execution of the Central Park Five, a group of teens of color falsely accused of sexually assaulting a white woman.

The story in question was written by me and appeared on the site BleacherReport.com about teams' fear of signing quarterback Colin Kaepernick, "the San Francisco quarterback" that Trump was discussing. One NFL team official told me "some teams fear the backlash from fans after getting him. They think there might be protests or . . . Trump will tweet about the team."

Trump exaggerated some aspects of the story (this will most assuredly shock you). The official quoted estimated that 10 percent of teams felt fans would revolt if the franchise signed him. Another 20 percent felt Kaepernick was no longer an effective player, while another 10 percent were mixed. The remaining teams, about 60 percent, did indeed "genuinely hate" Kaepernick for his peaceful protesting.

Nonetheless, for the first time in American history, a president publicly used sports and race as a wedge issue. It was a remarkable moment, but then, as now, these are remarkable times.

This particular Trump story, and others like it, along with Trump himself, are vital to telling the story of how NFL players, in just a matter of a few years, went from a group mostly averse to protesting and challenging the game and societal norms to aggressively doing so. The transformation of football players from drones to fearless fighters is mostly due to a handful of powerful forces: the rise of cell phone footage showing police killing unarmed black men; Kaepernick using the power of the NFL quarterback to raise awareness to that and other social justice issues; and, lastly,

Trump's opposition to Kaepernick and using the power of the presidency to cast a mostly black NFL player base as unpatriotic or, as Trump called them, "sons of bitches."

This story cannot be told without Kaepernick and Trump, in the same way the biblical story of man cannot be stated without Adam and Eve.

There are not two more opposite human beings than Donald Trump and Colin Kaepernick. Trump grew up privileged, white, and a New Yorker. Kaepernick was adopted, was born in Milwaukee, grew up in California, and is a lifelong football player. Yet in many ways—both bluntly and sadly—the NFL social justice movement would not have happened without Trump's racism and acrimony and Kaepernick's heroism and boldness.

It's not that Trump was the ignition source, but he was the instigator. Instead of attempting to calm and lead, he poked and smirked.

Kaepernick laser-focused on the issue of unarmed black men being killed by police. Then Trump, with an extensive history of racism and white supremacy going back decades, laser-focused on Kaepernick. The president's attacks on Kaepernick and NFL players energized those players, as well as large swaths of other Americans. There had never been a movement like this in the NFL before.

At another Trump rally on September 2017—this one in Huntsville, Alabama—the president again spoke about Kaepernick.

"We're proud of our country. We respect our flag," Trump said to loud applause. "Wouldn't you love to see one of these NFL owners, when somebody disrespects our flag, to say, 'Get that son of a bitch off the field right now?' He's fired! He's fired!'"

"Some owner's gonna do that. He's gonna say, 'That guy that disrespects our flag? He's fired. And that owner . . . they'll be the most popular person in this country. Because that's total disrespect of our heritage. That's total disrespect of everything we stand for." Trump then said something fairly stunning.

"If you see it, even if it's one player [kneeling for the anthem]," Trump said, "leave the stadium."

The problem is that Kaepernick wasn't on a team to be fired from. He'd effectively been blackballed by the NFL for kneeling during the national anthem, and that blacklisting of Kaepernick would continue until February 2019 (and then beyond), when a collusion grievance filed by Kaepernick against the NFL was settled by both parties. When Trump gave his second speech, he knew that Kaepernick wasn't even on an NFL roster, but the truth was irrelevant.

It was the second time the president had called for the firing of a sports figure. The first was when he said then ESPN anchor Jemele Hill, after she called Trump a white supremacist on Twitter, should be dismissed from the network. Trump's remarks about Kaepernick also came after praising white supremacists following a violent rally in Charlottesville, Virginia. Neo-Nazi protester James Fields Jr. drove his car into a crowd of anti-racist protesters, killing a woman named Heather Heyer and injuring thirty-five others. He was convicted in state and federal court of murder and sentenced to life in prison.

"It was cold-blooded. It was motivated by deep-seated racial animus," Thomas Cullen, US attorney for the Western District of Virginia, told reporters at Fields's sentencing hearing. He said

Fields's lethal car-plowing was calculated, calling it "a hate-inspired act of domestic terrorism."

"Charlottesville is never going to be the same," Cullen said. "It will be with this community, and the commonwealth of Virginia, and this country, for a long time."

Trump's handling of Kaepernick, as you would expect, was different from the words of the country's previous president, Barack Obama. "As I've said before, I believe that us honoring our flag and our anthem is part of what binds us together as a nation," he said at a CNN presidential town hall on September 28, 2016. "But I also always try to remind folks that part of what makes this country special is that we respect people's rights to have a different opinion.

"The test of our fidelity to our Constitution, to freedom of speech, to our Bill of Rights, is not when it's easy, but when it's hard," Obama added. "We fight sometimes so that people can do things that we disagree with as long as they're doing it within the law, then we can voice our opinion objecting to it but it's also their right."

Former presidential candidate Beto O'Rourke was actually one of the first politicians to support NFL protesters. He did it even before Obama, and while in the middle of a tough senate race in Texas against incumbent Ted Cruz. "Non-violently, peacefully, while the eyes of the country are watching these games," O'Rourke said. "They take a knee to bring attention and our focus to this problem to ensure that we fix it. That is why they are doing it. And I can think of nothing more American than to peacefully stand up, or take a knee, for your rights, anytime, anywhere, in any place."

The president's two outbursts about Kaepernick (and there were others from him on Twitter) exemplified how politics, race, and football were (and are) intertwined in what's become one of the most dangerous, and beautiful, times in sports history. Dangerous, because a sitting president used an athlete in particular, and sports in general, as an energy source for his bigoted politics. Beautiful, because, leading with Kaepernick, a group of heroic players stood up to the president.

That week was a particularly newsy one. There were the president's comments about Kaepernick in Alabama. The day after, the president announced on Twitter the de-inviting of NBA star Stephen Curry of the champion Golden State Warriors from the traditional White House celebration. Curry, who stated he would not be attending the ceremony as a form of protest before Trump removed his invitation, blasted the president, his policies, and his rhetoric. "Basically the things he said and the things he hasn't said at the right times, we won't stand for it," Curry said. "By acting and not going, hopefully that will inspire some change when it comes to what we tolerate in this country and what's accepted and what we turn a blind eye to."

"U Bum," LeBron James tweeted to Trump, "@stephencurry30 already said he ain't going!"

When James was later asked if he regretted calling Trump a bum, James said, "No."

NBA players weren't the only ones expressing their anger over the president's actions and rhetoric. Some NBA coaches spoke out as well. Two of them were the Golden State Warriors' Steve Kerr and the San Antonio Spurs' Gregg Popovich. Almost no coaches in the NFL, or other sports, publicly backed the players or objected to Trump's verbal maliciousness. They didn't out of fear of repercussions from ownership, or even the president himself, and certainly they were nervous about fan backlash.

Kerr and Popovich weren't worried about such repercussions in part because the NBA has a younger fanbase and definitely more progressive owners and front-office officials. They were also armored by winning. Kerr had just won a championship, and Popovich is one of just five coaches in the history of the league to win five. Neither man gave a damn as to what Trump thought about them—and it showed.

"Our guys felt pretty strongly even before we knew that we didn't have an invitation [to the White House, after winning the NBA Finals] that it was going to be a tough visit," Kerr told CNN in November 2017. "A lot of us, myself included, have been pretty critical of President Trump.

"I've been lucky to visit the White House with, I think, four different presidents, President Reagan, President Clinton, both President Bushes. I didn't always agree with their policy, but I never once thought, *Oh my gosh, I'm not going to go because I disagree with, you know, immigration or some foreign policy or tax reform.*"

"With all of those presidents that I mentioned, they were all above reproach in terms of their respect for their fellow man and their respect for the office. And I don't think any of us see that right now," Kerr added. "It's difficult to reconcile that and just say we'll put all that aside. You know, he can make fun of handicapped people, he can, you know, he can say a lot of, you know, nasty things, ugly things, whether it's about women or whomever."

Popovich, without equivocation or hesitation, has repeatedly taken jabs at Trump.

"This man in the Oval Office is a soulless coward who thinks that he can only become large by belittling others. . . . We have a pathological liar in the White House, unfit intellectually, emotionally, and psychologically to hold this office," he told *The Nation* in October 2017, "and the whole world knows it, especially those around him every day. The people who work with this president should be ashamed, because they know better than anyone just how unfit he is, and yet they choose to do nothing about it. This is their shame most of all."

That intense week also demonstrated the enormous differences (until Kaepernick) between NBA and NFL activism. The number of NFL players who spoke out against racism between Jim Brown and Kaepernick isn't long. The NFL, purposefully, attacks independent thinkers. It's not that the NBA didn't do that; it's just that it hasn't been as successful. The history of NBA players fighting fearlessly is long. Bill Russell, as a player for the Boston Celtics in the 1960s, challenged the commissioner to end player quotas since only two blacks were allowed on NBA teams at a time. Lou Alcindor was outspoken as any black athlete at the time, and did so initially, and bravely, as a college student at UCLA. "If you're in a racist society," he once said at a news conference, "and you're being discriminated against, it's up to you to do something for yourself." Oscar Robertson fought for improved conditions, pay, and free agency for NBA players and became despised for it by many fans and members of the media. At the 1964 All-Star Game, it was Robertson, along with fellow greats Elgin Baylor and Jerry West, who refused to leave the locker room unless owners provided increased salaries and benefits. Owners buckled. Decades later, one of the greatest three-point shooters of all time, Craig Hodges, wore a full-length dashiki to the George H. W. Bush White House ceremony celebrating the Bulls' title. After winning their second title, Hodges was released. The reigning three-point shooting champion, despite reaching out to every team in the league for years, never played in the NBA again.

LeBron James became the next cog in the chapter of the NBA player protester, leading the way for NBA players to make various statements after the killings of more unarmed African American men by law enforcement, like Trayvon Martin and Eric Garner. It was also James and other players who led the revolt to get racist owner Donald Sterling banned from the NBA after his taped comments became public.

One of the more remarkable moments in recent NBA history occurred on July 13, 2016, at ESPN's ESPY Awards as James, Carmelo Anthony, Chris Paul, and Dwayne Wade utilized their fame to draw attention to the myriad racial and social justice issues facing the nation. The speech is worth reading in its entirety:

> **ANTHONY:** Good evening. Tonight is a celebration of sports, celebrating our accomplishments and our victories. But, in this moment of celebration, we asked to start the show tonight this way—the four of us talking to our fellow athletes with the country watching. Because we cannot ignore the realities of the current state of America. The events of the past week have put a spotlight on the injustice, distrust, and anger that plague so many of us.
>
> The system is broken. The problems are not new. The violence is not new. And the racial divide definitely is not new. But the urgency to create change is at an all-time high.

PAUL: We stand here tonight, accepting our role in uniting communities, to be the change we need to see. We stand before you as fathers, sons, husbands, brothers, uncles—and in my case, as an African American man and the nephew of a police officer, who is one of the hundreds of thousands of great officers serving this country.

But, Trayvon Martin. Michael Brown. Tamir Rice. Eric Garner. Laquan McDonald. Alton Sterling. Philando Castile. This is also our reality.

Generations ago, legends like Jesse Owens, Jackie Robinson, Muhammad Ali, John Carlos and Tommie Smith, Kareem Abdul-Jabbar, Jim Brown, Billie Jean King, Arthur Ashe and countless others, they set a model for what athletes should stand for. So we choose to follow in their footsteps.

WADE: The racial profiling has to stop. The shoot-to-kill mentality has to stop. Not seeing the value of black and brown bodies has to stop. But also, the retaliation has to stop. The endless gun violence in places like Chicago, Dallas, not to mention Orlando, it has to stop. Enough. Enough is enough.

Now, as athletes, it's on us to challenge each other to do even more than we already do in our own communities. And the conversation, it cannot stop as our schedules get busy again. It won't always be convenient. It won't. It won't always be comfortable, but it is necessary.

JAMES: We all feel helpless and frustrated by the violence. We do. But that's not acceptable. It's time to look in the mirror and ask ourselves what are we doing to create change. It's not about being a role model. It's not about our responsibility to the tradition of activism.

I know tonight we're honoring Muhammad Ali. The GOAT. But to do his legacy any justice, let's use this moment as a call to action for all professional athletes to educate ourselves. It's for these issues. Speak up. Use our influence. And renounce all violence.

And most importantly, go back to our communities, invest our time, our resources, help rebuild them, help strengthen them, help change them.

We all have to do better. Thank you.

Across the entire NBA timeline, players took dramatic risks, stepping forward to force change. The current NBA player base was no different. "I was proud of the fact that they felt safe, within this league, to take political positions," said NBA Commissioner Adam Silver on the Showtime documentary *Shut Up and Dribble*.

But, back to that tumultuous week in July 2016. The president's stoking—he'd tweet about Kaepernick again the day after this Alabama speech—had set off battles all across the NFL.

One player tells a story of having his car being followed after leaving practice and subsequently hiring a private security firm for several weeks to protect his family and their home when he was away. Another remembers that as the anthem played and he knelt, someone from the stands yelled: "Fuck all you communist niggers." The player said a stadium security official heard the outburst and immediately removed the fan.

One of the least known aspects of the protest movement was the large amount of blunt racism players faced, in the open, during games as the protests unfolded. Terrelle Pryor was caught on video arguing with a fan in Kansas City, but Pryor maintains the argument was over him being called racial slurs by a fan multiple times. He posted on Instagram:

"Being called a nigger several times to the point where an NFL employee had to step to me and stand by me the whole game from second quarter on is the exact reason why guys are kneeling during anthem. I choose not to kneel because as a team we decided to be one and stand . . . but as I walked in tunnel hearing someone call me a nigger and say F word to me . . . me flicking the person off is more deserving . . . at some point you keep calling us the N-word we going to start acting up."

Inside at least one locker room, one player told me, there were arguments over Kaepernick and Trump that came close to fistfights.

In the fall of 2017, as his name became a living piece of history, Kaepernick did what he'd done since his NFL banishment. He worked out daily—lifting, running, and throwing. For the entirety of his exile, not a single team offered him a contract.

At one point, during the early days of his protests, I sat next to Kaepernick at his locker and asked him a number of questions. One of the first was, why was he doing this?

"I don't think America has seen anything like this in a long, long time," Kaepernick said, "and we can't sepa rate the NFL and America. They are basically mirror images of each other. The racism is more in the open now. It's going to get worse. It's going to get a lot worse."

That was in 2017. Three years later, we now know how right Kaepernick was. What we also know is that like the energized defenses of a body under attack from a viral invader, there was a national and massive resistance to Trump's racism, and much of that resistance started with Kaepernick and hundreds of NFL players. These were football's fearless fighters and their story is extraordinarily American.

Chapter 2

HATE MAIL

"Taking a knee during the anthem shows respect for the flag and for all those who fought and died for it and, at the same time, concern about problems within American society that need to be addressed. Pejorative and caustic comments about the practice show a disregard for one of the most important foundational principles of our great nation—freedom of expression—as well as ignorance of the corrosive impact of conscious and unconscious racial and class bias within our society."

—Former CIA Director John Brennan

So much of what football's fearless activists did is about the seen and unseen. Both were equally powerful and life changing for the players. The difference is, as you watched games and highlights and played fantasy football, you had no idea what was happening when the cameras were off and the interviews stopped.

One of those methods was how people angry over the protests communicated with the players. Those unseen interactions were vicious and at times frightening.

There are players who started protesting not long after Kaepernick began, and they also have stories to tell. They are stories of threats and acts of intimidation. They are stories of leaving social media because of numerous death threats, as well as being called "nigger" hundreds of times on Facebook, Twitter, and Instagram. The players talk of the personal and emotional toll resulting from their protests. They talk about how the impact from the threats and hatred still last to this day.

"It was draining," recalls one player, "constantly fighting off the racists on social media and worrying if any of them were going to come to your house or go after my wife or my daughter. All the players who protested will tell you that we weren't worried about ourselves. We were worried about the safety of our families."

Once players protested, played the game, and went home, the movement still weighed on them. They often worried that someone close to them might be harmed.

One NFL official, who works extensively with the league's security arm, estimated that over a three-year period, from 2016 to 2019, protesting players were targeted with approximately one hundred thousand racial slurs across various social media platforms. That same official said there were dozens of physical threats on social media—namely Facebook and Twitter—aimed at Colin Kaepernick and Eric Reid over that same period. Most of those threats, the official said, weren't deemed credible. "The people who did that were just guys with big mouths trying to scare Colin," this person explained.

But even if the threats weren't always actionable, the fact that athletes had to endure this was one of the unfortunate costs of their fight. This was part of the personal toll: *Was that a car following me*

or just going to same destination? Why is that person staring at me? Are
they carrying a weapon? Should I get personal security for my kids when
they go to school? Should I buy a gun?

Two players interviewed who took part in the protests said they
did purchase firearms. One said he bought a .38 caliber handgun
and a semiautomatic weapon. He purchased five thousand rounds
of ammunition and turned a part of his basement into a safe room.

Another player, a high-profile one who is still active, shared his
experience:

> There was something that happened once that really shook me,
> and it doesn't go the way you might think. It was about two or
> three months after I started taking a knee. A bunch of people
> got my email address, and the stuff people sent . . . it was bad. It
> was the kind of stuff that makes you really rethink just talking to
> people. I mean, people you don't know. For a long time, when I
> went [out] in public, I just kept my head down. I had never done
> that before in my life.
>
> One day, I got an email from a guy that started out very
> rationally. He disagreed with the protests because he was ex-
> Army and felt that we were disrespecting the military. That was
> bullshit—but he had bought that line. But it was respectful,
> until the end of the note. He said what really bothered him
> was the how the country didn't look like him anymore. He said
> his favorite quarterback was Johnny Unitas, and now all the
> quarterbacks were starting to "look like Colin."
>
> The whole thing scared me, but also made me really sad.
> There were a lot of people who understood and appreciated
> what we did. There were also a lot of people who didn't and
> didn't want to. We were scared of their ugly behavior and their
> potential for violence. But they were scared, too. They were
> just scared for different reasons. They were scared because
> black people, and black players, were showing we had power.

By showing we had power, it scared a lot of white fans, and people. We are one of the things that represented a changing country. The league is mostly black. A lot of star athletes are black. The president was black. I think when we started protesting there was a lot of fear. I think a lot of people who opposed us really just hated that the country was changing into a place they didn't recognize or want.

* * *

When players began sharing some of the emails they received, they were emotional to read. The hatred was startling. One player warned me that I might not be able to sleep for a few days. He was right.

A sample of some of the language used in the emails, and shared with me, appear below. The players did not want to be identified out of fear that sharing their names would only generate more correspondence. The language is shared solely to demonstrate the other side of the protest movement, the human side, the side where players weren't just risking possible career harm but physical harm as well.

"I don't know if everyone understands the mental part of what we were facing," says defensive lineman Michael Bennett, one of the first players to join Kaepernick's protests. "This is a big part of what happened. It's a part of what we had to overcome. I don't want anyone to feel sorry for us, just understand. People didn't just want to disagree with us. They wanted to stomp us. Some of them were violent, and they were urged on by [President] Trump. I don't think people get this at all."

"There were some scared players, bravely protesting," says one prominent player, "always looking over their shoulder, worried they were going to catch a bullet from the stands."

One player remembered that while kneeling during the playing of the national anthem played, he heard a loud bang and jumped. It was someone outside of the stadium setting off a firecracker, but the fear was real.

The tension, and sometimes fright over prospective violence, led some protesters to behave in extremely cautious ways. One player remembers getting a package sent to his house in which he didn't initially recognize the name. The package came after a series of threats he received over social media. After finally opening the parcel, he discovered that it was from a distant relative whose handwriting was unfamiliar. Inside was a note congratulating him on a play he made the previous week, and a framed photo of the play. But before deciding to open the package, he initially considered taking it to the police, thinking it might be a bomb.

In many ways, what some players faced was a campaign of domestic terrorism designed to intimidate them into not protesting.

Here is a small portion of some of those email messages those players received:

"You will die! White power!"

"Why do you niggers always want things handed to you on a platter?"

"Just shut up, you ungrateful black fucker."

"I followed your daughter to school today."

"You're un-American. I hope you fucking die."

"I hope you get raped in prison."

"You porch monkey socialist. I hope you get murdered."

"I hope you and your wife get beheaded by ISIS. You stupid sand nigger."

"Go back to Africa."

"You are disgracing our military. I hope you understand that you stupid trash."

"If I find out where you live, I'm going to bomb your house."

"What you don't get is that this is our country. This is Trump's country and you're just a nigger with a football."

"I hope you die like the nigger traitor that you are."

* * *

A protesting player remembers how snail mail from fans had increased twenty- to thirty-fold in the months after he began taking a knee. Once, after doing a visual inventory, a letter caught his attention, as on the back of the envelope there were three handwritten words: "Not hate mail."

He opened it, and there was a short paragraph written on notebook paper. "I know you get a lot of hate," the note said, "but I wanted to make sure you know a lot of us appreciate what you are doing. You are heroes. Thank you."

That note was sent in 2017. He still has it in his office desk at home.

* * *

"I was in eighth grade; the other guys were in high school," says Torrey Smith, who played for the 49ers, Eagles, and Panthers over nine seasons. "Just going down the street. Some guys were driving fast in the neighborhood, causing trouble. Next thing you know, the cops roll up, guns drawn . . . my hands are shaking in the air, standing in the street while they called for backup. I got searched down to my boxers. It was just guilt by association.

"I've always been the good guy: don't drink, don't smoke, don't do anything. But I've had guns drawn on me by the police three times in my life: college, high school, and middle school. And I still have little girls and kids walk up, point to me, and say, 'Hey, he's black.'"

"I remember back in high school, I switched to a different school for my senior year, and during our first game, the other team's crowd started yelling racial slurs at me before the game," says Titans safety Kenny Vaccaro. "I'm from a small, country town with a lot of people that aren't fond of black people. Even though I'm half-white and half-black, just being black in general has always made it more challenging when it came to a lot of things in life. It's made me a stronger person today."

Racism even effects players during the game. As Packers cornerback Damarious Randall told *Bleacher Report*'s Matt Miller in 2017:

Last year at the Dallas game. We were up early on, maybe 24–3, and you know how close the visitor sideline is to their fans. So it was almost like you could have a conversation with a fan. And just after every TD, I would celebrate and I get animated with fans. Then it was this guy every time we did something, I would celebrate and I would see him flipping me off. So after that, after every time we'd score, I'd look at him and ask, "What's up?" We were basically going back and forth then every time. Dallas started coming back, and I'd come sit on the sideline, and he'd be all up in my ear, trying to make it hostile. Long story short, after we won the game and made the FG, fans started talking and using the N-word. The same guy even threw his drink at me, which I dodged . . . if the drink had hit me, there would have been a brawl on the news. But I don't let what people say get to me.

* * *

"There were guys just nervous about their safety, their families' safety, and their careers," Michael Bennett said to me in 2018. "Can you blame them?"

There was reason for them to be worried. Rhetoric has consequences, and players knew this. The *Washington Post* reported counties that hosted a 2016 Trump campaign rally saw a 226 percent increase in reported hate crimes. This was over comparable counties that did not host a Trump rally. Words mattered, and players watch the news and read it like others. They knew what was happening in the country, and it scared them. In fact, at the height of the protests, in one 72-hour period, I loosely monitored the number of times on Twitter that Kaepernick was physically threatened. I stopped counting at 10,000. I also monitored the number of times he was called a racial slur. I stopped counting at 25,000.

* * *

Sometimes, the unseen is a letter sent to a player's home, and in other moments, the unseen is in the office of an NFL head coach.

It was the fall of 2016, and the protest movement was at its peak. Dozens and eventually hundreds of players were taking knees on football fields across the nation. What most people didn't know at the time (and still don't) was some players faced fierce pushback from their teams to stop protesting. In some cases, there was an implicit threat—keep protesting, and you'll lose your job. Indeed, one person actually did. His name is Antonio Cromartie.

Early in Cromartie's NFL career, he was viewed as a punch line. In 2010, Cromartie required a $500,000 advance on his Jets contract (he was traded to the team) so he could pay delinquent child support. He has fourteen kids by a number of different women.

Yet Cromartie was always so much more than that. He was a talented player who made four Pro Bowls during his 11-year career and is still credited for having the longest touchdown in NFL history—returning a missed field goal for a 109-yard touchdown. Cromartie was also extremely well respected in the locker room on each of the teams he played on.

By the time Cromartie got to the Indianapolis Colts in 2016, he was on his fourth team. Then, the protests started, and like many other players, they struck him on almost a chromosomal level. Like those also chronicled in this work, Cromartie had followed news of the police shootings closely. He'd become disturbed and saw the protests as a constructive—and meaningful—way to deal with that frustration.

The Colts, however, didn't see it that way.

During one team meeting then-coach Chuck Pagano asked the players to not take a knee. "When we got out on the field," he told them, "it's about football."

After Pagano said this, two players in the room looked at each other and rolled their eyes. They were astounded by what they felt was their coach's hypocrisy. The reason was Pagano had been diagnosed with leukemia in 2012 and his intensely personal story was talked about for years. The *Business Insider* called one of Pagano's postgame, post-cancer diagnosis speeches "one of the most inspirational postgame speeches you'll ever see." The Colts released video of the speech to the media.

It became one of the all-time feel good NFL stories and was so discussed a word emerged from it: Chuckstrong.

For Pagano, it wasn't just about football, and he discussed his cancer as an inspiration for others fighting the disease. For Kaepernick, Reid, Cromartie, and others, seeing unarmed black men killed by police was also extremely personal, and they were using their power as NFL players to bring awareness to what they felt was important. In some cases, it was personal for players because they knew some of the victims or knew friends and family who did. In other cases, it was personal simply because, like other African Americans, when someone is unjustly shot by police, one of the first thoughts is, *That could easily be me.*

For many people of color, all of this was extremely personal.

One of Cromartie's best friends, former Jets teammate Joe McKnight, was shot and killed by a white motorist who became enraged over how McKnight was driving. The driver, Ronald Gasser, lied when he said that McKnight lunged at him, forcing him to shoot, according to prosecutors. A jury convicted Gasser of manslaughter, and he was sentenced to thirty years in prison.

Cromartie first took a knee on September 18, 2016, before a Week 3 game against the San Diego Chargers. Colts team officials standing on the sideline told him to stand up, but he refused.

This is where the seen and unseen intersect in an unbelievable moment. As Cromartie was kneeling, a group of Colts employees surrounded Cromartie, attempting to block anyone from seeing him. Yes, you read that correctly: the Colts literally tried to shield Cromartie from being seen.

Cromartie says he was told not to kneel in the team's next game. He did anyway and was benched at halftime. He says that benching was solely because of his protest.

Cromartie did what Kaepernick had done before him. He protested knowing the ramifications would likely be the end of his career or, at the very least, the end of his tenure with the Colts.

Interestingly, almost a year to the day, on October 8, 2017, Vice President Mike Pence attended a Colts home game against the San Francisco 49ers. When several members of the San Francisco 49ers took a knee during the anthem, Pence and his delegation abruptly departed the stadium. Pence later tweeted, citing a trope that had formed on the right but wasn't accurate: "I left today's Colts game because @POTUS and I will not dignify any event that disrespects our soldiers, our Flag, or our National Anthem."

Pence also made a statement about his decision:

"I left today's Colts game because President Trump and I will not dignify any event that disrespects our soldiers, our Flag, or our National Anthem. At a time when so many Americans are inspiring our nation with their courage, resolve, and resilience, now, more than ever, we should rally around our Flag and everything that unites us. While everyone is entitled to their own opinions, I don't think it's too much to ask NFL players to respect the Flag and our National Anthem. I stand with President

Trump, I stand with our soldiers, and I will always stand for our
Flag and our National Anthem.

Then, Trump tweeted about Pence's actions. "I asked @VP
Pence to leave stadium if any players kneeled," Trump posted on
Twitter. "I am proud of him and @SecondLadyKaren."

One thing Pence failed to mention was the cost of flying from
Las Vegas to Indianapolis and then back west to Los Angeles,
a tab CNN said was $242,500—roughly $200K more than if
he'd simply flown from Vegas to LA. In a statement, a Pence aid
defended his boss's actions: "If the Vice President did not go to
Indiana for the Colts game, he would have flown back to DC for
the evening—which means flying directly over Indiana. Instead,
he made a shorter trip to Indiana for a game that was on his
schedule for several weeks."

What it all meant was, yet again, the Trump administration
was using football players as a political tool.

After his Week 4 benching, as he told *Bleacher Report's* Master
Tesfatsion, who first documented Cromartie's protest story, the
Colts released the Pro Bowl cornerback. There was little question
why the team took that action. It was because of the protesting.

"It ain't have nothing to do with my age, it ain't have nothing
to do with my style of play," he said. "It was because I took a knee."

Forty-seven players contacted over the past four years said
they privately faced similar pressures as Cromartie from either
a position coach, a head coach, a front-office executive, or a
member of the team's public relations department. One player
said a team lawyer contacted him after he started protesting and
asked him to "tone it down."

Another player said a general manager once pulled him aside after practice. "I like you," the player said the GM told him, "and I want you to have a long career in this league. But if you keep protesting, I'm not sure that will happen."

That's a great career you got there. Be a shame if something happened to it.

What's certain is there was a sustained—yet extremely quiet—attempt by large swaths of the NFL ecosystem to convince NFL players to stop protesting without publicly appearing to do so.

The bravery players demonstrated in the face of this pressure, opposing a slew of billionaire owners and standing up to the most powerful sports league in the country, is another part of their story that remains underappreciated.

The pressure on players from the NFL would only increase. And then, as some have said, when players failed to succumb, the NFL would go to another methodology:

Bribery.

But first, we need to answer a basic question: how did all of this happen? How did a group of football players help focus attention on the scourge of police brutality?

Before we can completely grasp and examine the alchemy and historic importance of the protest movement, how its reverberations continue to this day and will for decades to come, we first have to start with a quiet moment on a muddy football field in Santa Clara, California.

Chapter 3

ALTON STERLING

"As veterans, we implore all Americans to find your own way to challenge this status quo and advocate for 'a more perfect union.' Your method of protest may not be to refrain from the traditions surrounding our national symbols, and it doesn't have to be. You have the same right as Colin Kaepernick to choose whether and how to advocate, a right we support and served for. However you choose to use your voice, please do so with an understanding that many veterans do not condemn the protest of activists like Jackie Robinson, Colin Kaepernick and everyday Americans seeking justice. Indeed, we see no higher form of patriotism."

—An open letter from thirty five
military veterans to all Americans

Before Kaepernick became an almost household name and attracted the attention of the nation—and even parts of the world—the movement Kaepernick started was almost invisible. When Kaepernick began protesting at Levi's Stadium, no one outside of the team noticed. In fact, it only caught the attention of a few people.

"I had seen so much violence against black men by the police," Kaepernick once told me soon after he began protesting. "It built up. I thought as a society we were becoming complacent. We had a white supremacist running for president. There were black and brown men and women being killed, unarmed, by police, and there was little attention being paid to it."

How exactly it started remains one of the forgotten aspects of this story. There are actually two heroes who birthed the NFL's protest movement: Kaepernick and Eric Reid.

Reid was a teammate of Kaepernick's in San Francisco and like Kaepernick was distressed by the spate of police brutality. For Reid, as vital as that was, his activism was rooted in other things—like simple knowledge of American history. He never forgot it. He still studies it.

"Next year will be 2019. It will mark 400 years since the first slaves touched the soil in this country," he said at an October 2018 news conference. "That's 400 years of systemic oppression: slavery, Jim Crow, New Jim Crow, mass incarceration, you name it. . . . The New Deal set up what is known as the modern-day middle class. We didn't have access to programs—the G.I. Bill, Social Security, home loans—none of that. This has been happening since my people have gotten here. So I just felt the need to say something about it."

You see, most NFL players have historically been afraid to talk like this publicly. The owners, team executives, coaches, and league executives on Park Avenue pressure players directly, or indirectly, only to talk football. With a few exceptions throughout league history, like Jim Brown, most players kept quiet. Reid didn't.

A story by Bill Voth on the Carolina Panthers team website, where Reid was eventually signed after his protest, exemplified how the defenseman was perfect for the fight he would join. Reid's father, Eric Reid Sr., and his mother, Sharon Guillory-Reid, spoke to their son about blackness and all that it entailed. "First thing you gotta understand," Reid Sr. told Voth, is that "growing up as a black male in America, it's a difficult challenge."

"You are just as good as anybody else, no matter what color they are," the parents would tell their son. "So if you have any convictions . . . people not treating you right . . . you let us know. And you do what is necessary to correct that situation."

"They were taught," Reid said of his children, via Voth, "to respect the law, to be respectful to adults, and to stand up for what they believe in."

In other words, take no shit. Fight back.

However, Reid's parents weren't just talk. His father remembers an incident when Eric was in middle school and a teacher grabbed him by the neck. The next day, father and son were confronting the teacher and principal.

There were other lessons for Reid. While at LSU in 2011, he was stopped by police for turning around on a street that had been closed off for a concert. Reid told NOLA.com, "Then they left, and the original officer who stopped me came over and started screaming my Miranda rights in my face."

* * *

When Alton Sterling was shot six times by two white police officers in Baton Rouge, it was one of the most devastating moments of

Reid's life. Reid and his family were from Louisiana. "I felt like it could have been any one of my family members that live in Baton Rouge," Reid Jr. told NOLA.com. "It could have been my dad who works in Baton Rouge, and it could have been one of my brothers or sister. It brought me to tears and left me wondering what I could do to create change."

Reid was also direct proof that the primary lie used against protesting players—that they were anti-military—was propagandistic. The reason why he knew this to be true was because of his mother.

Sharon Guillory-Reid served six years in the Louisiana Army National Guard. In fact, Reid's family history is filled with those who served in America's armed forces. As Voth recounts, at least ten people from Reid's immediately family have served: a grandfather, who spent part of the 1950s in Japan; a great uncle, who was killed in the Korean War; another uncle, who spent thirty years in the Army with tours in Iraq and Kuwait; and a cousin, who served in Afghanistan.

"I just always tell him that he has my full support, that I love him, I'm supporting him. I'm behind him and I trust and I know that he's going to handle it in the way that he sees fit," his mother said. "All that he needs to know and to feel is that he has the support of his family."

"Not a single person in my family stated that [Reid's kneeling] was anti-military," she told Voth. "Every single person in my family sent me texts, Facebook messages about how proud they were and how they supported him. All of them were like, 'You can use my name. If anybody wants to talk to me, I'm active duty, I'm retired. Tell them to give me a call. We fully support him.'"

The murder of Sterling is something that still motivates Reid. Protests followed the shooting and the US Department of Justice requested a civil rights investigation. To Reid, he saw himself in Sterling.

"The biggest feeling I had," Reid told me, "was helplessness. I was angry and felt like I couldn't do anything. I was searching for a way to help. I felt like the message being sent to black men was black lives don't matter."

There's something else you must understand about Reid. Something he learned early on from his family was the value of loyalty and the belief in your values and principles. Reid had opportunities to reverse his stance in order to get an NFL job. He could have gone against his beliefs, but refused. In fact, the Cincinnati Bengals wanted him to do just that. In April 2018, Bengals owner Mike Brown and other team officials met with Reid, and Brown centered almost the entire conversation on the protests. Then, the owner told Reid he intended to prohibit protests during the anthem. He then asked Reid for his reaction to that.

Reid is not someone who is easily shocked, but he was stunned at Brown's brazenness. The moment wasn't just illustrative of how Reid was refusing to compromise his beliefs, it showed the cold determination many owners possessed at killing the protests.[1]

Kaepernick faced a similar situation that same month. ESPN's Adam Schefter reported on April 12 that the Seahawks had arranged for Kaepernick to fly to Seattle and work out for the team. These workouts are usually basic things. The player receives a medical

---

1   This was also after the Bengals' 7–9 season in 2017.

exam, meets with coaches and front-office executives, and then does a series of drills. In Kaepernick's case, he was going to throw a football as well. The Seahawks suddenly changed their mind when after asking if he planned to protest, Kaepernick said he would. The workout was suddenly postponed and then cancelled.

Perhaps, as much as anything, Kaepernick and Reid stayed true to themselves and their cause, because—and this might sound odd to some—they wanted to stay true to being black men. They started protesting to draw attention to the plight of people of color and to reverse course would be a betrayal of that cause. Also, they weren't going to be Michael Jordan.

> During his illustrious career, Michael Jordan rarely delved into issues of race. That was his choice, as not everyone is built for it. Jordan, however, went out his way to avoid the storm of race, and some in the media went along with his desire. In David Halberstam's *Playing for Keeps*, a biography of Jordan, Halberstam stumbled into a racial bear trap when writing about a meeting between Jordan and a Nike executive: "As Jordan smiled, race simply fell away," he wrote. "Michael was no longer a black man, he was just someone you wanted to be with, someone you wanted as your friend. The smile was truly charismatic. . . . It belonged to a man completely comfortable with himself and therefore comfortable with others. It seemed to say that only good things would now happen. More, it had a lift to it, a lift that carried ordinary people past their own prejudices. If Michael Jordan, he of the brilliant smile, was not burdened by the idea of race, why should you be burdened by it either?"

For Reid and Kaepernick, the notion of race "falling away," like a leaf falling from a tree, was absurd. Cops see race. The judicial system sees race. NFL owners see race. It is always there and impacts the lives of people of color on a daily, if not hourly, basis. It was as silly a notion as a postracial America after the election of Obama.

The two players weren't going to ignore the power of their cultural status during their sports life. They were never going to deny who they were.

How the protests began, however, remains one of the more fascinating parts of this story. Before the first preseason game of the 2016 season, Kaepernick sat on the bench during the pre-game national anthem. He didn't take a knee. Reid didn't notice. Neither did other teammates or the dozens of San Francisco media members. It wasn't until the third preseason game that the media finally did. Then, the country did—followed by parts of the world.

* * *

But there was one more thing Kaepernick wanted to do. He wanted to meet with former Green Beret Nate Boyer. It was Boyer who helped Kaepernick go from sitting during the anthem to kneeling. "He, you know, had sat on the bench," Boyer said in a 2016 interview with National Public Radio on how he and Kaepernick first came to speak:

> And I think it was actually his third time he'd sat on the bench. But it was the first time it had received national attention. And, you know, he got questioned about it, and he said, well, I'm not going to stand for the flag of a country that oppresses black people and people of color. And then he talked about, you know, social injustices and police brutality and why he thought, you know, he shouldn't be standing for the anthem.
>
> And it struck a chord with me, of course, and it struck a chord with a lot of people—a lot of people in the veteran community as well—because obviously the flag and the anthem and what that stuff stands for means something, you know, very different

to us. And I was pretty upset, you know, just because I felt like he didn't understand what those symbols really represent. And—but instead of letting my anger overwhelm me, I decided to relax a little bit, and I wrote this open letter that was just explaining my experiences, my relationship to the flag. And Colin actually reached out, said he wanted to meet with me. And we sat in the lobby of the team hotel, discussed our situation, our different opinions and feelings about all this. And I suggested him taking a knee instead of sitting even though I wanted him to stand, and he wanted to sit. And it was, like, this compromise that we sort of came to. And that's where the kneeling began.

Boyer served six years for his country and did multiple tours in both Iraq and Afghanistan. His military background added perspective to Kaepernick's methodology of how he was going to protest. Boyer also had a strong athletic background. He had never played organized football before attempting to make the University of Texas as a walk-on. Not only did Boyer get a roster spot, he became a starter at long snapper for 38 consecutive games and was named to the All-Big 12 Conference team. He spent one preseason in the NFL with the Seahawks.

"The idea is that taking a knee is more respectful," Boyer said in an interview. "When a fallen comrade dies, we stop and take a knee to honor him. I thought, and still do, that Colin taking a knee is respectful. I don't agree with it, but it wasn't being disrespectful to the flag or to soldiers."

Boyer then said something that remains at the core of Kaepernick's movement, something that was often lost as Kaepernick protested:

I think more than anything what my military service has informed me of is open-mindedness that I didn't necessarily have before, right? Before I even joined the military, for instance, I wasn't a very patriotic person. I just wasn't. You know, the reason I joined is because I went and did—I did some relief work out in the Darfur in the early 2000s, so I was in Chad and Sudan and at these refugee camps. And, you know, talk about oppression. And for that to spark this idea or this patriotism in me to want to fight for these people, to fight for those that can't fight for themselves. And, in my time in Iraq and Afghanistan, working with people that I have so little in common with cultures—and customs-wise—but I learned to respect them because I listened to them. We had these conversations to get to know each other, and we realized we want the same stuff. We're human beings at our core. And you put all those differences aside, and you don't care about the little things anymore. You know what I mean? And you fight alongside these people, and they become your brothers in arms as well.

We are more similar than we are different.

Kaepernick stopped sitting on the bench during the national anthem and began taking a knee after his conversation with Boyer. No one fully knew it at the time, but this silent protest would effectively end Kaepernick's NFL career. His attempt to bring awareness to the killing of American citizens at the hands of police was seen as hostile and un-American by NFL team decision-makers. It wasn't just that teams reacted to Kaepernick's protest. That would later be a particularly thorny factor, especially after media attention added kilotons of fuel to the protest's reaction. There were also a significant number of team executives—and the majority of owners—who hated what Kaepernick was doing. That fact was a big reason why Trump was able to gain traction inside the league: lots of NFL people agreed with him.

Again, in real time, this fact wasn't generally known, but the anger at Kaepernick was boiling quietly among many higher-ups in the NFL.

By taking a knee, Kaepernick's protests turned the football establishment on its head. His actions sent a specific message to the NFL. Kaepernick was his own man. The sport bred obedience. Kaepernick refused to comply.

He was an unlikely hero for the movement he began. He was a biracial child who grew up middle class and didn't have extensive or frightening contacts with law enforcement. Yet, in other aspects, Kaepernick was perfect. He graduated from Nevada with a 4.0 GPA and a degree in business management. He was also steeped in the history of American civil rights. He'd read dozens of books and engaged scholars on the subject years before joining the NFL. He closely followed the increasingly publicized and recorded stories of African Americans' deadly encounters with law enforcement. Months before his protest began, he started commenting on social media on some of the bigger cases of police brutality.

But there was another factor as well. Kaepernick wasn't compliant, or deferential, to the NFL power structure. "I feel like the NFL constantly tries to intimidate players and force players to bend to the will of the league," says Michael Bennett, brother of Martellus. "Colin didn't buy into any of that. He wasn't afraid of the owners."

The Bennett brothers were key cogs in the protest movement. Their popularity gave the protests thick credibility, and their bluntness was appreciated by players. One of the things Martellus did was ask white quarterbacks to join the protests. "If Peyton Manning joined the conversation, the conversation in the NFL would change," Bennett said at a forum in Washington, DC, called Athletes + Activism. "If Drew Brees came in and really joined the conversation, it would change. Tom Brady. All these great white heroes that they have running around, throwing the football—if they jump into the conversation, it would be so much bigger."

"If they were to take a knee with Colin Kaepernick, that conversation would totally change," Bennett said. "If Tom Brady took a knee, white America would be like, 'Oh my God. What is this that Tom Brady's talking about?'

"They would start doing research and would join in the conversation. It would pique their interest. But since it's a black guy taking a knee, it's like, 'Alright, these guys, here he goes again. It's another one of these guys out here doing this.'"

* * *

Most of all, Kaepernick was smart and studied, and believed that if people—especially people of color—weren't careful, history would again repeat itself. Kaepernick believed that ignoring the various grotesqueries of human history could lead to duplicating them.

Kaepernick argued to some 49ers teammates that not only was it wrong in failing to be more engaged in the fight for social justice but also it was dangerous to abstain from doing so.

By the end of September 2017, one year after the start of the protests, the kneeling started by Kaepernick had reached every corner of the NFL, many parts of the country, and even small corners of the world. On September 24, 2017, at a game in London, about two dozen players total on the Jaguars and Ravens took a knee. Across the NFL, by my rough estimate, that season saw almost 800 players protest in some form, with about half kneeling. The front pages of websites and newspapers led with the story. While those in the media industry—from movie stars to musicians—also knelt in various situations, it was those throughout the government who stood by Kaepernick who received the most attention. General Wesley Clark, a retired four-star general, publicly sided with Kaepernick. So did John Brennan, the former head of the CIA.

The year before, as Kaepernick kneeled every game, the largest number of players to kneel with him, from both teams combined, was nine. A year later, there were hundreds. President Trump, from the White House lawn, reiterated his opposition to the players kneeling. This only angered the players more. The story had become a full-blown chapter in the culture wars of the Trump era. The pushback against the players was at times frightening. In response to the Steelers team staying in the locker room during the anthem, a fire chief in a Pittsburgh suburb posted a video on Facebook, addressing coach Mike Tomlin: "Tomlin just added himself to the list of no good niggers. Yes I said it." The post became viral and the fire chief apologized, then later resigned.

A Missouri bar owner crafted a "Lynch Kaepernick" doormat at the bar's entrance. The director of the Michigan State Police called the players "millionaire ingrates who hate America and disrespect our armed forces and veterans" and are "a bunch of rich, entitled, arrogant, ungrateful, anti-American degenerates."

This of course was far from the first time Americans looked at protesters as wrongdoers. Republican pollster Frank Luntz recalled how a 1961 Gallop poll showed that 61 percent of Americans disapproved of the Freedom Riders taking desegregated buses into the segregated South. Also that year 57 percent of Americans said lunch counter sit-ins "hurt the Negro's chances of being integrated in the South." In 1964, 73 percent of Americans felt "Negroes should stop demonstrations now that they have made their point." In 1968, just before he was assassinated, a Harris poll showed King's *disapproval* rating at 75 percent.

Unintentionally, Trump empowered a new class of NFL athletes who wanted to shape society into a more racially tolerant place. Make no mistake: the NFL's protest movement represented one of the great power shifts in American sports history.

To be sure, this shift is part of a larger, familiar story about players attempting to find their way in a chaotic world. Except in the past, players mostly stayed in line, as owners and commissioners used their star power mostly to benefit the NFL, not the players themselves. It had been that way for decades. The wishes of the players were secondary. They were a product who were told what to do and when to do it, and any complaints led to lockouts, strikes, and even replacement players. For so long, the player base was scared. They were also aware of history. There were players strikes in 1968, 1970, 1974, 1982, 1987, and the owners locked out the players in 2011. In each one of those cases, the players lost their fight and were forced to relent, as the owners had more money and could simply wait them out.

"The players are like cattle, and the owners are ranchers, and the owners can always get more cattle," said the legendary president of the Dallas Cowboys, Tex Schramm, in 1987. That mentality toward the players has changed little in the more than three decades since it was first said.

Again, all of this history is vital. You can't understand the NFL player movement without first digesting the moments that led up to it. What Trump and others failed to understand was that athletes who had long been asleep when it came to social issues were suddenly awake. Kaepernick had started it. Trump had finished it. The movement was afoot.

"A quick thanks to the current occupant of the White House for energizing the social conscience of the modern American athlete," said Bryant Gumbel on HBO's *Real Sports*. "That occupant's . . . series of racist, churlish, and childish comments drew a variety of stunning rebukes and actions, which suggests jocks may finally be realizing that apathy won't cut it anymore. That in conjunction with their fame, they have important civic roles to play—especially now."

After Kaepernick was released by the 49ers and he waited for an opportunity to play again that wouldn't come, he watched Trump's hatred of NFL players—and their response from afar—not speaking publicly. One day, as the protests continued, he sat with his girlfriend Nessa Diab, a radio and television personality based out of New York, and an unsung hero of the movement.

Like Kaepernick, this moment would test her, and like Kaepernick, she refused to be crushed by it.

She knew, like Colin did, that the fight was just getting started.

Chapter 4

PAST IS PROLOGUE

"Abu Sa'eed Al-Khudri narrated that the Prophet, peace and blessings be upon him, said: 'Indeed, among the greatest types of Jihad is a just statement before a tyrannical ruler.'"

—Jami' at-Tirmidhi, *Book of Al-Fitan*, Hadith 2174

There have been previous moments in American history—many of them, actually—where racial fear was weaponized. The difference in the case of Colin Kaepernick is that the weaponization came from a sitting US president against a professional athlete. Not against a civil rights leader, or a freed slave, or even the fear of loss of Jim Crow, but a professional football player.

One of the few people to come close to how Kaepernick was treated was a man named Mahmoud Abdul-Rauf.

Muhammad "Mahmoud" Abdul-Rauf, born Chris Jackson, was the third overall pick in the 1990 NBA Draft by the Denver Nuggets. After converting to Islam in 1991, he officially changed his name in 1993.

The reason why Kaepernick's story sometimes may seem so familiar is because it's happened before. Kaepernick's story became a bigger one because Trump used the power of the presidency to try and stop Kaepernick. But Abdul-Rauf was Kaepernick before Kaepernick.

By the mid-1990s, he was one of the most devastating players in the league. Think Stephen Curry.[1] Similar to Kaepernick, he took a stance, despite having so much to lose.

Past is prologue, yes, and if you substitute his name for Kaepernick's, in some ways, the reaction of some in the public and media was almost identical. The issue became nuclear.

In 1996, Abdul-Rauf refused to stand for the national anthem, citing how the flag represented oppression and tyranny.

Initially, he stayed in the locker room and protested out of sight. A reporter's question, and subsequent story, ignited the entire situation. The late David Stern, one of the great innovators and top commissioners in any sport, nonetheless had an autocratic side. Like the NFL's Roger Goodell, Stern was extremely concerned with how advertisers would react. The money had to keep flowing, so Stern took steps to shut down Abdul-Rauf's protests before it picked up steam.

"What caused me not to stand was just my Muslim conscience, what I understood, and what I understand now," he said in the 2001 documentary *By the Dawn's Early Light: Chris Jackson's Journey*

---

1   "Never seen anything like Scurry? Remind you of Chris Jackson/ Mahmoud Abdul-Rauf, who had a short but brilliant run in NBA?" —Tweet by Phil Jackson, February 28, 2016.

to Islam. "I couldn't see myself, knowing the relationship that the US government had—and has—with what's going on in the world with starvation, with wars, with economical strangulation. With all of these things, I could not see myself, as an individual, stand for a symbol that represented that."

Stern suspended him and said Abdul-Rauf would be fined $31,707 a game. After meeting with the commissioner, Abdul-Rauf agreed to stand for the anthem if he could keep his head bowed and his eyes closed. Commissioner Stern agreed, and Abdul-Rauf's suspension only lasted a single game.

The public reception from Abdul-Rauf's stance may also sound familiar. Included in his documentary were numerous quotes and interviews from both players and fans reacting to his decision. Some NBA players understood that it was his right to voice his opinion, whether they liked it or not, such as Steve Kerr: "I don't necessarily agree with what he's saying, but I respect his freedom to express himself." Shaquille O'Neal said, "Muslims have different beliefs and have different anthems. You just have to respect that." There were even fans who took his side, as one interviewed at the time in Denver said, while wearing a red USA sweater, "I respect the fact that the man has principle. I may not agree with his statement—that's the irony of our freedom of speech. That you can say something I don't like."

And, of course, the other side had their say. Many jumped on similar narratives we've seen with today's activists. "I think it's an insult to all of the people that fought in the war and things like that, and it's an insult to America," said one fan interviewed at the time. Others felt that the decision was straight un-American.

"Ask Mahmoud if he'd rather not get paid in American dollars," screamed a fan at a Nuggets game.

At the end of the 1995–96 season, Abdul-Rauf was traded to the Sacramento Kings , where he saw his minutes drastically drop. After two years with the Kings, he became a free agent and received zero contract offers. He spent the next season in the Turkish Basketball League and elsewhere before returning with the Vancouver Grizzlies for 41 games in 2000–01. He was then out of the league and spent the rest of his playing career in places like Russia, Italy, Greece, Saudi Arabia, and Japan before retiring in 2011.

In a 2016 interview with *The Undefeated*, he put into perspective the message the NBA was sending to him, and what the NFL told Kaepernick. "It's a process of just trying to weed you out. This is what I feel is going to happen to [Kaepernick]," Abdul-Rauf said. "They begin to try to put you in vulnerable positions. They play with your minutes, trying to mess up your rhythm. Then they sit you more. Then what it looks like is, well, the guy just doesn't have it anymore, so we trade him."

"It's kind of like a setup," he continued. "You know, trying to set you up to fail and so when they get rid of you, they can blame it on that as opposed to, it was really because he took these positions. They don't want these types of examples to spread, so they've got to make an example of individuals like this."

When asked by the *Washington Post* if he saw similarities between himself and Kaepernick, he was quite clear:

No question. It's a duplicate pretty much. The hate mail, the attacks on his character, his personality, his race. "As an athlete, this is not what you should be doing. You should be either a social activist or an athlete." The same things. . . . This is why people, I guess, sometimes get upset when athletes speak out or actors or actresses speak out because they view us first as an athlete and a human second. No, I'm human being who happened to evolve into an athlete. And being a human being, the same thing that affects you affects me.

Similar to our fearless activists, there were death threats. When he and his family were building their new home, someone sprayed the letters "*KKK*" on a nearby sign. Later, after deciding not to move into it, the house was destroyed by fire.

Of the fans quoted, one rang out true to the underlying racism: "The pledge of allegiance to the flag of the United States of America does not vote for black people. I'm a Baptist, he's a Muslim. We still got black kids dying, and he's a black male that people look up to. And I'm just glad the brother took a stand."

"I don't feel like much has changed, if anything at all," Abdul-Rauf continued with *The Undefeated*. "Black folks are still being victimized disproportionately in the penal institution. It seems they are definitely disproportionately being shot and killed by policemen. Just overall the position that we are confronted with, and also being a Muslim, look at what Muslims are going through in this nation. I don't think really anything has changed, by and large."

After all the trials and tribulations, Mahmoud Abdul-Rauf has done his best to stay positive. "I want to live and die with a free conscience and a free soul when it's all said and done. That's the journey I'm on. I had to make that decision for myself and I found that after I did that, it took off a huge weight. Do you get ridiculed?

Do you hear the nonsense? Do people try to assassinate your character? Yes, but when it's all said and done, you're like, man, I feel good because I know that I'm standing on something that I believe in."

But, at the end of the day, race was again at the forefront for the vitriol he received. Unfortunately, he wasn't the only one.

* * *

Craig Hodges was one of the best pure shooters in the history of the NBA, winning three-consecutive three-point shooting contests (from 1990 to 1992). Like Kaepernick, he was excommunicated for his political views.

Hodges became disgusted by what he saw as a systemic oppression of African Americans in society and believed using his power as an athlete was a way to fight that oppression. He urged Bulls teammates to boycott the first game of the 1991 NBA Finals to bring attention to the lack of black coaches in the league. Then, after the Bulls won the title and made their visit to the White House—then under the leadership of the George H. W. Bush administration—Hodges wore a dashiki to the event, and hand-delivered a note to the president. It read:

> The purpose of this note is to speak on behalf of the poor people, Native Americans, homeless and, most specifically, the African Americans, who are not able to come to this great edifice and meet the leader of the nation where they live. This letter is not begging for anything, but 300 years of free slave labor has left the African American community destroyed. It is time for a comprehensive plan for change. Hopefully, this letter will help become a boost in the unification of inner-city youth and these issues will be brought to the forefront of the domestic agenda.

Decades later, in an interview with Slamonline.com in 2019, Hodges sounded almost exactly like Kaepernick on why he took the actions he did. "You have a chance in this life to make choices," he said. "The choice that I made was: I wanted to be on the right side of history. When people are oppressed, somebody has to stand up."

Following the 1991–92 season, and coming off his second straight championship, Hodges went unsigned. No team would return his calls or offer him a tryout. This came in the wake of his actions at the White House when he handed Bush that note. Not long after that, he was gone from the NBA. Hodges, to this day, still asks a question: just how free are people of color?

"It was something that we had to have a firsthand approach on, not a second," says Hodges. "We can't be sitting around, watching. We have to put our lives into the movement if we want it to sustain itself and to get to the point where we get solutions as opposed to continuing to have conflicts about the same issue."

Following the 1991–92 season, and coming off his second straight championship, Hodges went unsigned. No team would return his calls or offer him a tryout. This came in the wake of his actions at the White House when he handed Bush that note. Not long after that, he was gone from the NBA. Hodges, to this day, still asks a question: just how free are people of color?[2]

---

2 "I also found it strange that not a single team called to inquire about him. Usually, I get at least one call about a player we've decided not to sign. And yes, he couldn't play much defense, but a lot of guys in the league can't, but not many can shoot from his range, either." —Phil Jackson to Ira Berkow of the *New York Times* in December 1996.

Chapter 5

MAGNIFICENT

"Easily one of the most talented quarterbacks that I've ever seen."
—Packers quarterback Aaron Rodgers,
during a 2017 interview with the author

A consistent criticism of Kaepernick still repeated to this day was that he was never a good player (and thus not worth the attention he was getting). In fact, this criticism was (and is) the most persistent. There's a clear reason why. By diminishing Kaepernick's football abilities, his impact off the field could also be dulled.

The problem is he *was* good. Really good. Even people inside the sport who didn't like his protests admitted this. It was undeniable, and one of the people who saw his talent up close was coach Jim Harbaugh. The moment Harbaugh benched starting quarterback Alex Smith and went with the young Kaepernick, it changed the trajectory of Kaepernick, Harbaugh, the 49ers, the NFL and, in some ways, the twenty-first century social justice movement.

Harbaugh believed Kaepernick had star potential. It turns out, he was right.

* * *

Jim Harbaugh had long been a creative coach. He was named Coach of the Year while at Stanford, and his offenses were often the most potent—and imaginative—in college football. This was no different when Harbaugh coached the 49ers. The team wasn't just creative, it was physical and smart. In his first season, the 49ers lost to the Giants in the NFC Championship. The next year, on November 11, 2012, they began the season 6–2, but then lost starting quarterback Alex Smith to a concussion.

Before Smith's injury, the former No. 1 overall pick was third in the league in passer rating (at 104.1) and first in completion percentage (at 70.0). When Smith recovered from his injury two weeks later, rather than taking back his place in the starting lineup, Harbaugh stuck with the hot-handed Kaepernick, who had 360 yards and three touchdowns—including 76 rushing yards with a touchdown—in Smith's absence.

"One of the things about Colin is he's extremely smart and a fast learner," said Harbaugh to me in 2018. "I felt comfortable he could lead us. The other thing is that you have to remember that time. The offenses we ran weren't as common in professional football as they are now. Plus, no team had a unique talent like Colin."

Translation: Harbaugh believed Kaepernick would be able to do things because of his rare physical talents in an offensive system the league rarely saw. It would be like interjecting an unstable element into a balanced ecosystem.

As much as Harbaugh liked Smith, who had been the team's starter since being drafted in 2005, he saw Kaepernick's ceiling as higher—and he was right. Kaepernick could run what was essentially a college offense, mixed in with the pro concepts, and he could also throw from the pocket with accuracy. Defenses had a difficult time defending against his multifaceted game and, to Harbaugh, he could use creative play calling to maximize the young quarterback's abilities.

Kaepernick finished the rest of the season as the team's starter, and Harbaugh's gamble worked: the 49ers finished the regular season with an 11–4–1 record. In just seven starts he had passed for 1,814 yards and 10 touchdowns, had 415 yards rushing, 5 rushing touchdowns, only 3 interceptions, and a passer rating of 98.4.

In his first game as a starter on November 19, 2012, in Week 11 against the 7–2 Chicago Bears, he completed 69 percent of his passes and threw for 243 yards and two touchdowns with zero interceptions. The 49ers won the game, 32–7.

In the few games where he struggled from the pocket, he'd rely on his legs, leading the team in rushing (or close to it). Then, in another contest, like the one against the New England Patriots in Week 14 (where he threw four touchdown passes) he'd sit comfortably in the pocket.

"I felt we had a really good team, and Colin fit in well as the starter," said Harbaugh in 2018. "He could do almost anything. The big thing, again, was how smart he was. Also, he was so calm. That's not common for young players."

That calmness, as well as his extraordinary talents, were on display in the most explosive game of Kaepernick's career. It happened against the Packers on January 12, 2013 in the divisional round of the playoffs. It is, to this day, talked about as one of the more remarkable playoff performances by an NFL quarterback in league history.

Kaepernick rushed for 181 yards—an NFL record for a quarterback. His two rushing touchdowns were on runs of 20 and 56 yards. He also went 17-for-31 for 263 yards and two passing scores. His quarterback rating was 91.2.

Kaepernick's speed always seemed to shock defenders, which is understandable. After all, he's 6-foot-5 and weighs 230 pounds. Players that tall—especially quarterbacks—aren't supposed to run that fast. But he did.

There had been quarterbacks like Kaepernick before, such as Fran Tarkenton, Michael Vick, Steve Young, Randall Cunningham, and others. Kaepernick was simply bigger, stronger and faster. He wasn't new age—he was an upgrade, the newest iPhone.

This was why Harbaugh had made the change. This was why he took the risk.

Kaepernick's dealings with the media after being named the 49ers' starter were often low-key encounters. He didn't brag and rarely spoke of himself, only his teammates. After that playoff game, however, Kaepernick couldn't help but be publicly overjoyed. He lowered his defenses and when asked about how his tenure as a starter had gone thus far, Kaepernick smiled.

"It's been amazing," he said. "I couldn't ask for anything more."

* * *

There's something else you need to know about Harbaugh's decision to stick with Kaepernick once Smith was healthy. There were players in the 49ers' locker room that hated it.

"We respected the decision that he made," tight end Vernon Davis said at the time. "A lot of guys weren't happy about it, but we had to respect it."

The reason was because of an old NFL belief system that goes as follows: when a player is injured, he gets his job back. There are exceptions, but this is the general rule. So when Smith was benched and wasn't named the starter after his concussion symptoms subsided, it angered some teammates.

Kaepernick knew this, and one of the more unknown stories is just how much—and how quickly—he became not just well liked but also respected by his teammates and the locker room. "He worked as hard as anyone," Davis says now. "He made sure people understood he wasn't taking his starting position for granted. He was tough and smart. I don't think people get that tough part. They saw his athleticism, but he took some shots, got back up, and kept going. Players really respected him for that."

Teammates of Kaepernick's also spoke of his mental toughness, which was on full display in the NFC Championship Game against the Atlanta Falcons on January 20, 2013.

The 49ers trailed 24–14 at halftime. In the locker room, as Harbaugh addressed the team, some players turned their gaze to Kaepernick, attempting to see how a large deficit in such a big moment was impacting hm. But Kaepernick was placid and attentive.

In the second half, he showcased the other part of his game, which was throwing from the pocket. His throws were sharp and accurate, and with each score, the 49ers' confidence rose. The comeback was almost anticlimactic. Everyone in the stadium seemed to know it was inevitable. The 49ers certainly did. They won, 28–24, as Kaepernick went 16-for-21 for 233 yards, one touchdown, and just one sack. He rushed twice for 21 yards and had a 127.7 passer rating.

Kaepernick was twenty-five years old. He'd played in just two career playoff games. In the first against the Packers, he rushed for 181 yards and two touchdowns. The yardage set a new NFL record for quarterbacks and set a 49ers record for rushing in a post-season game regardless of the position. In his second game against the Falcons, he had a 127.7 passer rating. Yes, Kaepernick was playing with a formidable 49ers defense, one of the best in the league, and yes, at times, his throws could be wildly inaccurate. Yet he was only in his second year and had already amazed large swaths of the football world.

* * *

While his journey as an NFL quarterback was just beginning then, just a few years later, he was in a remarkably different place. He'd not only become a veteran pass thrower, he'd also become a symbol. One of the questions that's often asked is why did so many players follow Kaepernick's lead once his protest started drawing attention? Part of the answer is our current political climate. Players believed President Trump was a threat, and the safety of people of color, perhaps their very lives, was more at risk because of the racism he was generating. His policies, like trying to eliminate social safety nets and attacking Obamacare, were also mostly detrimental to people of color, at least in players' minds.

"I think in locker rooms all over the league, a lot of black players were angry over Trump," says Reid. "But guys were tired of complaining. When Colin and I started protesting, we provided a place where players could express themselves. It was mostly about social justice issue and police shootings, but it was also about Trump."

There was also a simple and key belief that the continued police shootings had reached an alarming level.

The answer is also in the game of professional football itself. Inside the 49ers' locker room, Kaepernick was popular and well liked. But he was also the same away from the game. For years, Kaepernick grew his base of friends across the sport. There was also a sense of pride for black players seeing a black quarterback excel the way Kaepernick did. There were still, at that time, few black throwers in the league.[1]

In all, Kaepernick used the cred he built up with excellent play on the field, and the respect he earned off it, to generate trust with players around the NFL. He was a familiar face to players once the protests started.

"Everyone knew Colin or about him," says Pro Bowl defensive back Richard Sherman, who for over a decade has been one of the most respected players in football. "He was respected by a lot of guys. Players knew if Colin was doing this, it was from the heart, and something they could get behind."

After the Falcons game, and with the 49ers on their way to the Super Bowl, the locker room was joyous and chaotic. Players

---

1   Of the 31 teams (not including the 49ers) in the 2012 season, only five had an African American quarterback start the majority of their games: Washington (Robert Griffin III), Philadelphia Eagles (Michael Vick), Carolina Panthers (Cam Newton), Tampa Bay Buccaneers (Josh Freeman), and Seattle Seahawks (Russell Wilson).

were hugging and celebrating. Kaepernick was also elated as he put on a white hat and pulled a T-shirt over his shoulder pads; both had the word "Champions" etched on them. Kaepernick enjoyed the moment, but he was already thinking about New Orleans, the location of Super Bowl XLVII—the biggest game of his life. This is what all great players do. They are always, no matter the moment, thinking several steps ahead.

Reporters gathered around his locker. One asked Kaepernick how he felt.

"Just excited," he said, "to keep going."

* * *

It was the fourth quarter . . . 34–29 . . . 4 minutes and 19 seconds left in Super Bowl XLVII. The ball was in Kaepernick's hands.

Before that moment, Kaepernick had steadily moved San Francisco's offense downfield. At one point, Kaepernick accounted for 23 of the game's 26 second half points. Kaepernick finished the game with 302 yards passing and 62 yards rushing. He joined legendary 49ers Hall of Famer Joe Montana as the only two quarterbacks to pass for 300 yards and run for more than 50 in a Super Bowl.

On fourth and goal at the five, Kaepernick aimed to the back right corner of the end zone. Crabtree was held, and the pass was slightly long as Kaepernick was hit in the chest by linebacker Dannell Ellerbe just as he released the ball. That essentially ended the game with the Ravens winning 34–31.

It's been written here before, and should be repeated, that it was often stated by people who didn't like Kaepernick that he was never that talented. Yet he had practically carried the entire 49ers' offense on his back. Or, those same people said he was selfish prima donna. But after the game, he stood at the podium, and took the blame for the loss.

"I feel like I made too many mistakes for us to win," Kaepernick, wearing a dark suit jacket and matching tie, told reporters after the game.

Not long after the game ended, Kaepernick was on the flight home, and he could only think, in that moment, about one thing:

How could he get better?

* * *

"When I first saw Colin play," says Russell Wilson, "I was amazed by him. He was one of the most talented guys I ever saw play the position. He still is. Our teams had some serious battles, and I know our defense always loved the challenge of playing against him."

Kaepernick entered the 2013 season as the starter as the 49ers traded Alex Smith to the Kansas City Chiefs for two second-round picks (in 2013 and 2014). There was no question now; this was Kaepernick's offense.

San Francisco's first two games of the 2013 season were against two of the best young throwers in football. The opening game was versus Aaron Rodgers and the Green Bay Packers at home, and Kaepernick, in another moment that demonstrated just how talented he was, outdueled Rodgers.

Kaepernick threw for 412 yards and three touchdowns while Rodgers had 333 yards, three touchdowns and one interception.

The 49ers won, 34–28. "There were times," Rodgers said to me in 2018, "when he was just unstoppable."

The next week, however, he was stopped, as the Seattle Seahawks beat the 49ers, 29–3. While Kaepernick had played well against the Packers, the Seahawks' defense was packed with speedy, athletic, and smart players who knew how to slow the nimble quarterback. The Seahawks in fact were one of the few teams that had the formula for stopping Kaepernick. They used fast linebackers and defensive linemen in pursuit to cut down his escape routes and running lanes, and made him throw the ball as much as possible. Then the Legion of Boom would be waiting. The Seahawks won easily, and would go on to capture 11 of its next 12 games.

On December 8, 2013, the 49ers would get revenge for their Week 2 loss to Seattle, beating them with defense, as well as some precision throws from Kaepernick. That win was an ignition source, and the 49ers won their last six regular-season games to finish the year at 12–4. Since the Seahawks won the division, the 49ers had to play their first playoff game on the road, meaning Kaepernick would again be facing Rodgers.

Rodgers always liked and appreciated Kaepernick as a player and, later, as the face of the protest movement. Rodgers was, and is, one of the most thoughtful and progressive players in the sport. He was also one of the few white players who expressed public support for Kaepernick. "I'm gonna stand because that's the way I feel about the flag—but I'm also 100 percent supportive of my teammates or any fellow players who are choosing not to," Rodgers told ESPN's Mina Kimes in 2017. "They have a battle for racial equality. That's what they're trying to get a conversation started around. I think he should be on a roster right now. I think because of his protests, he's not."

This was a vital moment because Rodgers wasn't just one of the few white players to publicly back Kaepernick, he was also one of the most powerful voices in the league.

Every summer, I travel to various NFL training camps and interview players and coaches. The Packers have been a frequent stop, and I've had the pleasure of sitting with Rodgers at his locker and talking football. He's engaging, smart, and extremely opinionated. Once, I asked him what he remembered about Kaepernick. "He was fearless and just a good player," said Rodgers. "I know our defense really respected him."

Then Rodgers paused. "You could see, even when he was young, that he was a great leader. He was special."

Chapter 6

BRIDGES

"What should horrify Americans is not Kaepernick's choice to remain seated during the national anthem, but that nearly 50 years after Ali was banned from boxing for his stance and Tommie Smith and John Carlos's raised fists caused public ostracization and numerous death threats, we still need to call attention to the same racial inequities. Failure to fix this problem is what's really un-American here."

—Kareem Abdul-Jabbar, in an August 2016 guest editorial in the *Washington Post*

Colin Kaepernick as a player has been compared to other quarterbacks throughout history, including Minnesota Vikings' Fran Tarkenton, Atlanta Falcons' Michael Vick, and San Francisco 49ers' Steve Young. Some of those comparisons are accurate. The comparisons that were rarely accurate related to how his activism was described off the field. He was called a twenty-first-century Malcolm X by some or a modern Jim Brown by others, the latter one of the more outspoken athletes of his generation. There were also comparisons to Muhammad Ali and Jackie Robinson.

But none of those comparisons were truly accurate. The most accurate one is almost never made. It's Paul Robeson. He was one of the black athletes who bridged the past to the present.

Robeson was a remarkable trailblazer in football, and his hallmark was using the same toughness he unleashed in the game to fight racism off the field. There was no turning of the other cheek. This part of his personality was explored by Rich Shea, who wrote in *Rutgers Today*:

> As a first-year student at Rutgers College during fall 1915, when Paul Robeson was the sole African-American student on campus and only the third to be enrolled in the 149-year-old school, he held a white classmate over his head in rage and thought he wanted to kill him. But he didn't. After Rutgers' football head coach George Foster "Sandy" Sanford shouted, "Robey, you're on the varsity!" Robeson placed his new teammate—the one who'd just stomped on his hand in an attempt to break it—on the ground unharmed.

When he tried out for the team, as Shea documents, he was assaulted by white players who were also attempting to make the roster. They broke his nose and dislocated his shoulder. He considered quitting football, but thought back to something his father, a former slave, once told him. "I wasn't just there on my own," Robeson told a reporter in 1944. "I was the representative of a lot of Negro boys who wanted to play football and wanted to go to college, and, as their representative, I had to show that I could take whatever was handed out."

Added Shea:

> "One game during his junior year was emblematic of Robeson's prowess. Playing against Newport Naval Reserve, an undefeated

team comprising 11 All-Americans, Robeson scored one of the two Rutgers touchdowns while on offense. But, he was so dominant on defense, which held Newport to just one first down, that Newport felt like it was up against 11 Robesons, according to one reporter's account. After Rutgers upset Newport, 14–0, yet another reporter called him 'a veritable Othello of battle'—a moniker foreshadowing the eponymous role he would famously play a decade later."

What Robeson later did was use the popularity he gained as being the best football player of his time as a propellant to fully engage in the fight for civil rights.

Kaepernick began to understand, toward the end of his NFL career, that athletes had immense power and that power could be used to bring attention to issues that were particularly important to African Americans. But also, he knew athletes have influence that others, including entertainers, and even some politicians, did not. Not everyone could act or sing or be president but everyone could hit a baseball in their backyard or shoot hoops down the street.

For much of the early twentieth century, Paul Robeson was among the most famous black men in America. He was a singer, movie star, athlete, lawyer, and activist who blasted America's foreign policies—especially on the continent of Africa—as well as how blacks were treated in America. His public embracing of the Soviet Union and communism made him a prime target during the McCarthy Era.

When Robeson was dragged before the House Committee on Un-American Activities, which was determined to destroy him, he didn't back down an inch. He was defiant and strong.

"The reason I am here today, you know, from the mouth of the State Department itself is: I should not be allowed to travel because

I have struggled for years for the independence of the colonial peoples of Africa," he told the committee, as documented by Howard Bryant in his book, *The Heritage: Black Athletes, a Divided America, and the Politics of Patriotism.* "I stand here struggling for the rights of my people to be full citizens in this country, and they are not. They are not in Mississippi. And they are not in Montgomery, Alabama. And they are not in Washington. They are nowhere, and that is why I am here today."

In the way Robeson was hauled before congress and called un-American, Kaepernick has been hauled before right-wing media, and a sitting president, and social media is filled with millions of people saying Kaepernick doesn't love his country, hates cops and the military, and should be kicked out of the country. The attacks on Robeson, including the revoking of his passport, annihilated his ability to earn income and essentially destroyed his livelihood; Kaepernick lost his job as a football player.

Also, and perhaps most important, the way Robeson fought racism and the Red Scare on behalf of every black person in America, Kaepernick has engaged a similar fight against police brutality on behalf of black and brown people.

They are twins separated only by the decades but conjoined with a universal message: our lives matter, and we won't be silenced—even it costs us everything.

* * *

The NFL is approximately 70 percent black. Its black stars, like Russell Wilson, Cam Newton, Patrick Mahomes, Lamar Jackson, Deshaun Watson, and a host of others are household names. They are marketed and cherished in a sports league that is the most powerful in the nation. In the NFL today, like in the NBA, black players dominate.

But, of course, it wasn't always this way. Before America embraced black talent, the nation shunned it. Yet black football players continued to fight for acceptance, and the distant relatives of those men are key cogs in a sport that has become the most important in this country's history.

What Wilson, Newton, Mahomes, and others show is how the power structure has changed. The biggest example of this is the prevalence of the black quarterback.

Tom Brady and Drew Brees dominate the position, but some of the league's biggest stars are black quarterbacks. They follow huge stars like Randall Cunningham, Warren Moon, and Donovan McNabb.

The quarterbacks are a large reason why people love football so much and why its impact is so significant, attracting heads of state, religious leaders, advertising executives, kindergarten teachers, and presidents.

Today's African American players follow in the footsteps of those before them. There was Duke Slater, the greatest African American football player before World War II and, easily, the greatest player of the 1920s. The first African American man to coach an NFL team, Fritz Pollard, did so in Akron, Ohio, a city that had the highest Klan membership in the country.

There was Joe Lillard, a running back for the Chicago Cardinals, whom the media nicknamed "The Midnight Express." In 1933, he scored almost half of the team's points on the season. One year before, in the third game against the Boston Braves, Lillard played running back and quarterback, returned kicks, and used a drop kick to score an extra point. The headline to the story on that game in the *Boston Globe* read: "Negro Star of the Chicago Eleven Thrills 18,000 by Dazzling Runs as Cardinals Down Boston."

The struggles of African Americans are a part of the NFL that people don't remember or even know. A number of men fought racial quotas, the Klan, and brutal racism to make the NFL what it is today.

They would fight, but even the power and will of those men couldn't stop what was an unofficial—but enforced—ban on black players, from 1933 to 1946.

Then, following the ban, three things would happen. One year before Jackie Robinson broke the color barrier, two African American players were signed by the Cleveland Browns (Bill Willis and Marion Motley), and another by the Los Angeles Rams (Kenny Washington), ending the ban on blacks in the NFL and making them the first African Americans in the modern era to play professional football.

On December 28, 1958, the Baltimore Colts beat the New York Giants in the NFL Championship. It was the first playoff game to go into sudden death overtime and is known as "The Greatest Game Ever Played," perhaps the biggest turning point in the evolution of the popularity of professional football. The game was broadcast nationally on NBC. Forty-five million people watched, and to many football historians that game would mark the official beginning of the NFL's steady climb to American sports dominance.

Wrote author Michael MacCambridge in his book *America's*

Game, "By the end of the Colts-Giants game, a seismic shift in the American sports landscape had clearly begun. In another decade, after another New York football team and its charismatic leader stunned the sports world, football was no longer the rebel, but the new king. And baseball was no longer the national pastime."

Also, in the late 1950s and into the 1960s, someone would come along and change everything forever. He would transform the image of the black football player, transform the sport, and even change Hollywood. His name was Jim Brown.

* * *

What's old is new again, part one million.

Gale Sayers was a legendary running back for the Chicago Bears. He made the Hall of Fame, the 1960s All-Decade Team, the 75th Anniversary All-Time Team (at both running back and kick returner), and the 100th Anniversary All-Time Team. He is one of the most decorated players the NFL has ever produced.

He was drafted in 1965 but, one year before, in an act of courage, Sayers took part in a protest at his school, the University of Kansas. Before protesting, he'd been advised by friends and others that participating in the sit-in might hurt his draft prospects. He didn't care.

A news story documented the sit-in:

> All-American halfback Gale Sayers, who is closing out his career at the University of Kansas before entering pro football as a member of the Chicago Bears, made what amounted to perhaps his final major gesture toward racial justice on the U-K campus. The outspoken star was arrested after he joined 110 students in a

sit-in demonstration outside the office of Chancellor W. Clarke Wescoe in the University's Strong Hall, to demand an end to racial discrimination in fraternities, sororities and university-approved housing.

Said Sayers, in explanation of his protest against campus: "They accept me as a football star, but not as a Negro."

* * *

The power of the NFL, unparalleled now, can be traced to a handful of people and moments throughout league history. One of those names, unquestionably, was Jim Brown.

Brown did not care what you thought. He did not want to fight racism quietly. Or politely. He wanted to kick it in the teeth.

The 1960s saw several significant events in the NFL, but none matched the historic magnificence of Jim Brown. No player, event, or moment eclipsed Brown's dominance of the sport during this decade. The 1960s saw him not just lead on the field but also transform into football's first civil rights activist, the first black action hero in cinematic history, the first NFL player who fought for union rights, and the first player to openly fight against discriminatory ownership practices.

There is no single category into which Brown neatly fits. He is the football star who was cheered by hundreds of thousands of Cleveland fans, yet was not allowed to eat in the same restaurants with them. He was a movie star, yet a loner. He loved women, yet physically and mentally abused a number of them. He was confident and powerful, yet sometimes insecure. He was dedicated to helping the downtrodden, the poor, the imprisoned, giving perfect strangers a helping hand, yet at times has been strangely distant from his own flesh and blood.

The irony of Brown is that while he would later become a critic of Kaepernick and a supporter of Trump, it was he who was one of several black athletes from that decade who laid the groundwork for athletes like Kaepernick. Only Muhammad Ali was a bigger influence on the modern NFL player.

After Brown, the NFL would enter an era of progress and expansion unlike it had ever seen before—both on the field and off. It would see the first black head coach in the modern era and the first black Super Bowl quarterback. The sons of bitches, as Trump called NFL players, were prospering.

* * *

But there is more history—much more. So much of this history is about black men overcoming the brick walls constructed in front of them, particularly at the quarterback position. The league now is full of black men playing the position, like Baltimore's Lamar Jackson and Kansas City's Patrick Mahomes. But the people who paved the way faced extraordinary challenges and bigotry.

One of those men was Marlin Briscoe. Briscoe was drafted by the Denver Broncos in 1968, becoming the first starting black quarterback in the AFL. He faced extreme racism from fans and players which, to no surprise, took immense emotional and physical tolls, something noted by Hall of Famer Gene Upshaw in William C. Rhoden's book *Third and a Mile*.

"He never really had a chance because in those days, they didn't give you a chance," Upshaw said. "You're in the moment, and you don't have a point of reference because there's no one else in front of you. Being a pioneer is a bitch."

Another one of those men was James Harris. He played at Grambling for legendary coach Eddie Robinson. It was clear that Harris, with a booming arm and remarkable smarts, was an NFL-caliber player. But there was still that little racism problem. No black man had ever started at professional quarterback in the National Football League. Robinson believed Harris could be the first.

There would have to be preparations, however. Harris practiced with Grambling staff for potential NFL and media interviews. Speak softly, they told him. Smile, they said. Don't ever appear too angry.

On the field, Robinson made sure that Harris didn't run the 40-yard dash for teams. Harris was fast, and if he ran a quick forty, teams would want to switch him to either wide receiver or defensive back.

Harris was drafted in the 8th Round (192 overall) by Buffalo and started for the Bills in 1969. A year later, after the AFL-NFL merger, he became the first African American quarterback to start an NFL season. Throughout his tenure there, the Bills put him in a $6 a night room in the YMCA, away from his teammates in a hotel during training camp. At a local mall, teammates would walk by Harris without acknowledging him. Then came the death threats and hate mail. One of several messages Harris saved read: "Now that you pickaninnies no longer dance for us on street corners it is only right that you do so in stadiums. . . . We will be at the Raiders game to watch you do your act for us, 'boy.' [Signed,] White America."

A headline in the *New York Times*, before a Bills game against the Jets, read: "Jets Are Likely to Face Harris, Bills' Negro Passer, on Sunday."

When Harris left Buffalo to play for the Los Angeles Rams, the death threats continued, becoming more intense. This one was particularly specific and frightening. Someone said they were going to shoot him as he ran out of the tunnel. "One time during the '75 season, Shack got a death threat," remembered former teammate Ron Jaworski. "This is at the Beverly Hilton Hotel, where Rosenbloom used to invite friends like Johnny Carson and Jonathan Winters and Sammy Davis Jr. to hang around with us at the buffet the night before a home game. Well, I get up to our room, and Shack is clearly nervous. He tells me some club officials just told him that they were beefing up security because of a death threat. Not to make light of it, but I told him maybe I should ride to the Coliseum with [running back] Rob Scribner—the Rams couldn't afford to lose both quarterbacks."

"That was the longest night of my life," Harris remembered. "We had security outside the door. They escorted me to the game. Man, I ran through that tunnel to the field as fast as I could. I don't remember much about the game. But I do remember running fast through the tunnel on the way out."

All of this is history you must know. You cannot understand or decode what Kaepernick was doing without it. Kaepernick is all of this history, and all of those events, in the body of one man. He took on the POTUS. He brought attention to social justice issues that would have likely been ignored by large swaths of America.

Polling shows that to African Americans, he is a hero, viewed as positively as Muhammad Ali.

Kaepernick was also a catalyst—not just for football but other parts of sports and American society. Trump's election led to mass pop culture resistance, and that resistance found its way into the NFL bloodstream. Musician Rihanna refused to perform in the Super Bowl LIII Halftime Show in support of Kaepernick. Beyoncé took a different approach, using Super Bowl 50 to pay tribute to the Black Lives Matter movement. Jay-Z, before he became a part of the NFL's PR machine, rapped how he rejected an opportunity to perform at the Super Bowl:

> I said no to the Superbowl
> You need me, I don't need you
> Every night we in the endzone
> Tell the NFL we in stadiums too

* * *

The year was 1982. The history books won't show it as one of the most vital years in league history, though it symbolized a remarkable turnaround of African Americans in a sport that spent decades shunning them. That year was the last one where African Americans were the minority in professional football.

It was a stunning transformation and demonstrated the persistence, courage, and talent of the African American athlete. Yet, there was still one gigantic problem. They were being prevented from two glamorous positions: quarterback and head coach.

One of those firsts happened in 1989, when Art Shell was named the first black head coach in the modern era, and the first since Fritz Pollard in 1921. The firsts continued in the 1980s and 1990s. On January 31, 1988, the same Washington team that only decades earlier refused to allow black players on it, was now embracing Doug Williams. He was the quarterback in Super Bowl XXII and had just led the team to a 42–10 blowout of the Denver Broncos. Williams' statistics: 18-for-29, 340 yards, and four touchdowns. He was named the game's MVP. Williams was the first black quarterback to play in a league championship game or Super Bowl. Like James Harris, and a number of black quarterbacks before him, Williams had suffered numerous indignities and death threats.

More black quarterbacks played in the NFL in the 1990s alone than the previous seventy years of professional football history.

* * *

Racism is insidious. It is one of the ugliest of diseases. It impacts everyone—even those who should know better. Even a liberal, open-minded white NBA player like Kyle Korver. A story he wrote for the *Players' Tribune*, titled "Privileged," showed how even someone like Korver, a model citizen, can succumb to the virus.

On April 8, 2015, NBA players Thabo Sefolosha and teammate Pero Antic—members of the Atlanta Hawks—were arrested outside a New York City night club. During the altercation, NYPD officers broke Sefolosha's right leg. His Hawks were about to make the playoffs, but he would miss them when he needed to have surgery eight days later to repair a fractured tibia and ligament damage.

While arrested for being in the wrong place at the wrong time, Sefolosha refused to accept a plea bargain and instead took the case to court . . . where he was found not guilty of all charges. He would end up suing the city—as well as the eight police officers who broke his leg—for up to $50 million in damages. He would end up settling for $4 million, donating a "substantial amount" to the nonprofit organization Gideon's Promise.

In his piece, Korver shared a look into his unconscious bias:

> When the police break your teammate's leg, you'd think it would wake you up a little.
>
> When they arrest him on a New York street, throw him in jail for the night, and leave him with a season-ending injury, you'd think it would sink in. You'd think you'd know there was more to the story.
>
> You'd think.
>
> But nope.
>
> I still remember my reaction when I first heard what happened to Thabo. It was 2015, late in the season. Thabo and I were teammates on the Hawks, and we'd flown into New York late after a game in Atlanta. When I woke up the next morning, our team group text was going nuts. Details were still hazy, but guys were saying, *Thabo hurt his leg? During an arrest? Wait—he spent the night in jail?!* Everyone was pretty upset and confused. Well, almost everyone. My response was . . . different. I'm embarrassed to admit it. . . .
>
> It didn't take long for me to figure out that Thabo was one of the most interesting people I'd ever been around. We respected each other. We were cool, you know? We had each other's backs.
>
> Anyway—on the morning I found out that Thabo had been arrested, want to know what my first thought was? About my friend and teammate? My first thought was: *What was Thabo doing out at a club on a back-to-back??*
>
> Yeah. Not, *How's he doing?* Not, *What happened during the arrest??* Not, *Something seems off with this story.* Nothing like that.

Before I knew the full story, and before I'd even had the chance to talk to Thabo . . . I sort of *blamed* Thabo.

In many ways, Korver's words were a byproduct of Kaepernick's actions. Kaepernick didn't start the conversation on race and policing, but he did intensify it. Along with the Black Lives Matter movement, he modernized it, and the vibrations from his words reached everywhere.

Football doesn't want its quarterbacks being political because they are the face of the franchise. The NFL wants them to be plain. Anything else, to a lot of owners, teams, and league officials, is simply unwanted.

* * *

As the public debated the protesting and President Trump kept launching volleys from the White House—practicing his brand of "moral vandalism" as presidential candidate Cory Booker once coined it—black players had to live their lives off the field. Their money and power offered little protection from the post-Trump election America, where racial tensions were on the rise.

Jonathan Casillas got his football start at a high school in New Jersey. He was so good he received a football scholarship from Wisconsin. After playing four years and graduating with a degree in Agricultural Business Management, Casillas went undrafted (due to an injury, forcing him to miss the Combine). He would sign as an undrafted free agent with the New Orleans Saints and go on to have a successful career. He's a thoughtful player, and football has provided him a good life, but he says there is one inescapable fact that money and power cannot change:

At the end of the day, I'm still gonna be a black man in America. I'm thirty years old, I drive a Mercedes. When I get in my car and a cop gets behind me I'm very, very nervous. Don't know why. It was the same exact thing when I was sixteen, seventeen years old. Still to this day, get in my car, I have a daughter in my car, I don't have anything illegal on me. I'm not doing anything illegal. I'm not drinking or driving, I don't do stupid stuff like that. But a cop gets behind me, I am so nervous. And I have been pulled over for no reason. And when they find out I'm a Giants player they start a conversation with me. That's happened to me several times, in recent times that's happened to me. Throughout my career, I don't know, it's happened to me so many times I can't count. I'm tired of being a target. I'm going to try and change all of this.

In April 2017, Delanie Walker took an eight-day overseas trip to the Middle East to visit military members as part of a USO tour. None of that seemed to matter after Walker kneeled during the national anthem on September 24, 2017. After that, Walker and his family received death threats. Trolls found the Instagram account of Walker's young son and sent him threatening messages. Walker's team, the Tennessee Titans, decided to provide a security detail for his family.

"I'm not going to change who I am," says Walker. "I'm still going to trust people and help people. But this America scares me. I think we as players can make it a more understanding place."

There isn't a more cautious player in football than Russell Wilson. He is almost cartoonishly corporate, but something about these times has changed almost everyone in the sport. In a 2017 team meeting, Wilson spoke up in some of the strongest terms about why players must be engaged in changing America. Wilson explained why to the Seattle media that year:

The overall gist of it all was: You know … I've been fortunate to have my own kids now, and see other players on our team have kids. And different races and people. I think about our huddle. I think about when I go into the huddle there's 10 other guys in the huddle, and there's all different races. There's black guys. There's white guys. There's guys from other locations and different socioeconomic statuses who grew up different. But we all share one common cause, and one common goal: We all want to win, and we all want to make a difference in our communities.

Really, for me, I was passionate about it because I am really concerned about what's next, for our future, for our future kids and what we are going to do for the people who are going to lead this world one day. I pray for my kids every day that when they go to school that racism isn't a thing that stops them from going where they want to go. And it's not just my kids. It's your kids. It's everybody's kids. I think that's really critical. That was on my mind. That was on my heart, especially.

* * *

It would be a lie to say things haven't gotten better for athletes of color. They are making massive amounts of money; what Lebron James once called "generational money." The racism, however, is still ever-present and strong—like a resistant bacteria, but it's power in sports has eroded. There's no longer a question of *if* there will be a black NFL head coach, but how many. There are NFL quarter-backs of color, and they are, in fact, the stars of the NFL. Yes, they still face double standards. Bill Polian, a Hall of Fame executive who built multiple Super Bowl teams, said on ESPN in 2018 that Lamar Jackson should move to wide receiver. "Short and a little bit slight," Polian said. Jackson is 6-foot-3.

"Clearly, clearly not the thrower that the other guys are. The accuracy isn't there," Polian said, which was also false.

Jackson would face other issues once his NFL career began, and the double standard some black quarterbacks face was evident to the Ravens' coaching staff. What led John Harbaugh to start Jackson was a multigame losing streak late in 2018 and an injury to starter Joe Flacco.

Before making a final decision on whether he should name Jackson the permanent starter, John called his brother Jim, who faced a similar situation with Kaepernick. Jim said that Kaepernick brought a certain type of energy to the team, and their 49ers' coach wanted to keep that energy, so he benched Alex Smith and went with Kaepernick. John told his brother he felt the same way, and, the following day after that conversation, Jackson was named the starter.

Harbaugh was prepared for the challenge of such a young starter entering the lineup at the most crucial of positions. He wasn't, however, prepared for the additional scrutiny black quarterbacks face.

Suddenly, John was getting racially tinged questions from some in the Baltimore media, on a nearly weekly basis, about Lamar's throwing accuracy, his knowledge of the offense, his ability to learn, how long he could last, and other similar topics.

John had been the head coach of the Ravens since 2008 and had led the team to victory in Super Bowl XLVII (against the 49ers). He'd seen everything and built considerable relationships with area media. Yet one source described how John felt that suddenly people he respected, or thought he did, were asking him questions about Lamar he believed were racist or, at least, incredibly disrespectful.

John spoke privately about how the treatment of Jackson opened his eyes about what black quarterbacks faced and, in a larger sense, opened his eyes to the racism black people face overall.

"John really wants Lamar to stick it up the ass to all his critics," one source said, "to have a Hall of Fame career. Of course that will help him win, but for John now, part of it's personal. He wants Lamar to prove a point, and he wants him to open doors for other black quarterbacks who can hurt you outside and inside the pocket."

Jackson is part of a long line of black quarterbacks who faced double standards and even had to take steps to diminish their running abilities, so they weren't switched to a different position. Warren Moon tells the story of purposefully running a slow 40-yard dash at his pro day so teams thought he was slow and wouldn't try to move him to defensive back or wide receiver. Harris made sure not to even run the forty for the same reason.

Thankfully, this is no longer an issue. In fact, after Jackson's MVP performance during the 2019 season, and Patrick Mahomes's MVP performance in Super Bowl 2020, it's highly arguable that Jackson, an African American man, and Mahomes, a biracial one, are the cofaces of the league.

To say that we've come far in professional sports when it comes to issues of race is an understatement. Yet it's also staggering just how far we *haven't* traveled. A story in a 1991 *Sports Illustrated* issue reviewed an earlier *SI* story, written in 1968, on the plight of the black athlete. The 1991 story demonstrated how little had changed from 1968, and aspects of both stories, despite the growing acceptance of black athletes in the twenty-first century, showed how much has stayed the same since both of those articles were published.

"The first article in the (1968) series was titled 'The Cruel Deception' and slapped readers immediately with a quote from the athletic director of the University of Texas at El Paso," wrote the 1991 story, "who had an unusually large number of black athletes on his teams and who actually thought he was being quite fair-minded when he said, 'In general, the nigger athlete is a little hungrier, and we have been blessed with having some real outstanding ones. We think they've done a lot for us, and we think we've done a lot for them.'"

* * *

What is old is new again, part one billion. On a Wednesday—August 28, 1963—250,000 people marched on Washington in one of the largest rallies for human and civil rights in American history. It was also where Martin Luther King Jr. gave his speech commonly referred to as the "I Have a Dream" speech. To this day, the protest—and King's speech—are one of the most iconic moments in the battle for civil rights and one of the most important in American history.

Yet what was equally astounding was how opponents of civil rights framed the march. Two days after its conclusion, the *Mobile Register* newspaper in Alabama wrote an editorial that encapsulated the feelings of a large swath of the country. The language is extraordinarily similar to what has been said about Kaepernick and the protesters now. The editorial was titled: "Intimidation March An Irresponsible Act":

The ill-conceived "civil rights" intimidation march on the

nation's capital cannot be reconciled with the sensible way of presenting a grievance. It was directly in conflict with good judgment and common sense. A mass outpouring that seriously disrupts operations of the federal government itself for a whole day does not logically come within the constitutional "right of the people peaceably to assemble and to petition the government for a redress of grievances."

This is how some at the time felt the movement should be handled. It should be done with minimal consternation, and inoffensive to whites. There was a time and a place, blacks were told. Decades later, when NFL players began protesting, they would hear the exact same message.

Chapter 7

FAKETRIOTISM

> "There are plenty of heroes in this country that Nike could feature. But a Castro-loving, cop-hating, ex-three-year backup quarterback is not one of them."
>
> —Fox News' Sean Hannity, on Nike's Kaepernick campaign

An important thing to remember is that the attacks on Colin Kaepernick, and other protesting players, have yet to stop. Kaepernick is still villainized by a large part of the media. He is still a target. It's likely he will be for the rest of his life.

In July 2019, the pregame speech of a Connecticut minor-league hockey coach named John Krupinsky went viral. In it, Krupinsky blasted anyone who did not stand for the anthem as un-American. "We are not women's soccer," he said. "We are not the NFL. If there is anyone here who is going to be disrespectful to either the American or Canadian National Anthem, grab your gear and get the fuck out now because you will never see the ice in this arena."

Krupinsky was of course referring to Kaepernick but also to

Megan Rapinoe, the captain of the US Women's Soccer Team, who in 2016 took a knee during the anthem in solidarity with Kaepernick. It happened during the National Women's Soccer League match between the Chicago Red Stars and Seattle Reign FC. After that moment, Rapinoe became a hero to numerous protesting players, including Kaepernick. Rapinoe was like the players. She had a great deal to lose, and little to gain, but felt the protest was necessary. "Being a gay American, I know what it means to look at the flag and not have it protect all of your liberties," Rapinoe said at the time. "It was something small that I could do and something that I plan to keep doing in the future and hopefully spark some meaningful conversation around it."

Krupinsky's speech has over seven million views, and after it became public, he was a star with right-wing media. His appearance on *Fox & Friends* typified the argument used against Kaepernick. "I take pride in my country," said Krupinsky, who is also an officer with the Danbury Police Department. "I've unfortunately seen it cover too many coffins. I think we can take a timeout to give two minutes' worth of respect to our soldiers, to our firemen, to your policemen. I don't think that's asking too much. I'm not going to apologize for asking players to show a little bit of respect when it's either the American or Canadian national anthem."

Krupinsky was another person who either accidentally or purposefully ignored the players' message. They weren't protesting the anthem, the military, the police, firemen, Martians, Vulcans, or anything else. They were using the moment to bring attention to their communities on an issue that mostly impacted people who looked like them.

The attacks on the players were also sometimes less direct but equally threatening. The second incarnation of the XFL began in February 2020. The commissioner of the league, Oliver Luck, father of the retired Colts star quarterback Andrew Luck, declared that no players would be kneeling during the anthem. "Players will stand and respect the flag," he said on the *Bloomberg Business of Sports* podcast. When asked what would occur if they didn't, Luck responded, "There'll be consequences." (One consequence for the XFL was that it folded in 2020.)

We haven't seen that type of threat or authoritarianism in professional sports for some time, and people like Luck still failed to understand what the players were doing. "No matter how much we said we weren't protesting the anthem," says Kenny Stills, "people accused us of protesting the anthem. They just didn't want to listen."

This was one of the key frustrations of football's fearless activists: people simply refused to listen. Players pleaded time and again, but within a large section of the American population the facts just didn't matter. In some cases, players even spoke directly to the fans and other Americans with their own words. That's what happened when then Houston Texans offensive tackle Duane Brown and Eric Reid both wrote op-ed pieces for *Sports Illustrated* in July 2016.

Brown is one of the unsung heroes of the fearless activists. He fought with protesters from the beginning, and, like many other players, put his career at risk. In October 2017, when NFL owners met in New York to figure out ways to deal with the protests, Texans owner Bob McNair, according to a report in *Sports*

Illustrated, equated the players to prisoners who needed to be controlled by the wardens. "We can't have the inmates running the prison," McNair was quoted as saying.

The comment incensed players from the around the league—especially those on the Texans. Almost all of the players took a knee during the anthem, including Brown. Several days later, the All-Pro tackle was traded to Seattle. As he wrote for *Sports Illustrated*:

> I am a football player, but I am not just sticking to sports. The events of recent weeks in America should force all of us to have difficult conversations in our locker rooms, in our homes and in our workplace about the root causes of violence, hatred and racism in our country. We have an obligation as professional athletes who give back so much to our communities to educate ourselves and be part of these important discussions.
>
> The narrative created by people who do not understand it would lead you to believe that Black Lives Matter is a radical, police-hating mob. Not only is that viewpoint wildly incorrect, but it also oversimplifies and trivializes the real prejudices that black people endure at the hands of some police officers. Saying "Black Lives Matter" is not saying that the lives of black people matter more than the lives of others, it's saying our lives matter EQUALLY to everyone else and when they are taken unjustly, we expect justice. That is part of the movement's stated mission.

Krupinsky wasn't the only one still framing Kaepernick as anti-Patriotic. A United States senator, and a senatorial candidate, did the same exact thing.

Bradley Byrne, running for a senate seat in Alabama, ran a campaign ad in the winter of 2020 portraying some left-wing politicians—and Kaepernick—as divisive forces that hated the military and were tearing the country apart.

"It hurts me to hear Ilhan Omar cheapening 9/11," he said in the ad. "Entitled athletes dishonoring our flag. The Squad attacking America." As he spoke in the ad, images of Kaepernick, Omar, Alexandria Ocasio-Cortez, Rashida Tlaib, and Ayanna Pressley appear on screen.

After the attack on Iran's top general, Qassem Soleimani, in January 2020, Kaepernick tweeted that the attack fit a pattern of "American terrorist attacks against Black and Brown people for the expansion of American imperialism."

South Carolina senator Lindsey Graham in January 2020 was asked about Kaepernick's tweet during an interview on the Fox News show *Sunday Morning Futures.*

"He's a loser on and off the field," Graham said of Kaepernick. "It's un-American. He's a racist. If you're looking for racism in America, Mr. Kaepernick, look in the mirror."

The idea of Kaepernick as a racist was an interesting twist, especially considering that it was Graham, while running for president in 2015, said of Trump: "He's a race-baiting, xenophobic religious bigot. He doesn't represent my party. He doesn't represent the values that the men and women who are wearing the uniform are fighting for."

Fox News host Megyn Kelly also chimed in, again, "Because everything is racist. Everything," she tweeted sarcastically on January 6, 2020. "Even fighting back against terrorists who kill Americans. Nike, feeling proud?" Kaepernick was the face of Nike's campaign to celebrate its thirtieth anniversary.

It's not that people wanted politics out of sports. It's that they only wanted *their* politics in sports.

Yes, the attacks on Kaepernick were continuing, some four years after he began protesting. Nonetheless, Kaepernick was still inspiring people as much as he was angering others. One of many who saw Kaepernick as a hero was Kelly Holstine.

Holstine was one of a handful of people given a Teacher of the Year award from the Council of Chief State School Officers and Education Minnesota. The teachers were honored during the NCAA national championship football game in January 2020. They were recognized before the singing of the national anthem. Then when the anthem began, Holstine took a knee.

"Like many before, I respectfully kneeled during Nat'l Anthem because, 'No one is free until we are all free,'" she later wrote on Twitter, referencing Kaepernick and citing an often-used quote from Dr. Martin Luther King Jr.

At the game were President Trump and First Lady Melania Trump.

* * *

One night, as the players and the protests grew exponentially—as did the coverage of them—Fox News' Tucker Carlson ran a banner on his show that headlined one segment on the protests. The banner read, "Flag Under Attack."

Of course, the players weren't protesting the flag, or the anthem, or police, or later, as some accused, first responders. The players were using the anthem as an opportunity to draw America's attention to the problem of violence against citizens at the hands of law enforcement. Players stated this repeatedly but, to the conservative media, it didn't matter.

The protests were viewed differently along racial lines—not just political ones. How one views the protests depends, like many other movements or politics in general, on the media consumed. A CNN poll showed that 59 percent of whites said the players were wrong to protest in the manner they did, while 82 percent of blacks said it was right. Ninety percent of Republicans disagreed with the protests while 72 percent of Democrats backed the players.

* * *

The players' fight for social justice is destined to be messy and thorny. All civil rights battles are. Ali was despised when he declined to enter the Vietnam War and spoke against the racial injustices of the time. Now, he's revered by most Americans. The same, one day, will happen to Kaepernick.

But the messiest part of pursuing inalienable rights is often that pits the crusaders against the police. This is the trickiest part for players, who continue to emphasize that they are not anti-police. The juxtaposition of players wanting police to be accountable for their actions, and conservatives thinking the police are practically infallible, was destined to lead to friction. It was also going to change how NFL players were viewed by the public.

"One of the things I thought after I heard about Colin taking a knee," says Michael Bennett now, "is first how brave he was. Then I thought, 'This is gonna change it all for NFL players. I don't think the NFL will ever be the same again.'"

* * *

There is one final difference between players today and players from the past and between the Trump era and past presidential ones. One player said the difference is rooted in "Faketriotism."

"I mean no offense to any players from the past," said one offensive star, "but we're not fooled by the league any longer. They can't use us as props for war and faketriotism."

I heard this term used privately several times by players—faketriotism. What did it mean to them? "Athletes are used to sell the military," one player said. "Our star power is used to promote war."

This is obviously a remarkably sensitive topic, but it is one that, again, was mentioned repeatedly during the height of the anthem protests and still shapes the opinions of some players now. There is a history here, and it is one that played a factor in both the protests and the evolving history of the new, more socially strident NFL player. History is important here. History is king, and the players are well aware of it.

The recent history players know, and incorporated into their thinking when it came to the protests and living during these times, started in November 2015. It was called "paid patriotism." The Department of Defense paid the NFL—and other professional leagues—millions for large flags to unfurl on the field before games, flyovers of military jets, and the acknowledgment of military personnel before games and at halftime. Again, it has to be noted that the military paid the NFL, not the other way around. The players received none of that money. The Patriots, Bills, and Baltimore Ravens all received over $500,000. The Browns got ten grand. The Saints received approximately $475,000.

Once it became public that the money was accepted by the NFL, the league, embarrassed, returned it, some $700,000 in May 2016. The incident wasn't over for the players, however. For many of them, these events stayed imprinted on their minds.

Players are often thought of by fans—and even some in the media—as mindless gladiators. Well, they aren't. They are sophisticated and, in many ways, better historians than the average fan.

The NFL has long been political. That is often the part of today's NFL that is lost on the viewer. For decades, the league has used its political clout to, in particular, back America's war efforts. The 1960s saw a great amount of cultural upheaval, and football wasn't shy about throwing elbows in that volatile environment. Like now, the league leaned right, and like now, it was often against the wishes of its players. Former commissioner Pete Rozelle put the NFL on the record as supporters of the Vietnam War. He sent some of the game's biggest names on goodwill tours to Vietnam. Rozelle, as *Sports Illustrated* notes, mandated that players stand upright during the anthem, hold their helmets under their arms, and disallowed "talking, nervous footwork, gum chewing and shoulder-pad slamming."

One player spoke up against the Rozelle's mandates, and that was Cardinals linebacker Dave Meggyesy, who openly protested the anthem. Meggyesy was a unique figure in league history. He spoke openly and brazenly about the violence of the sport and its impact on the body. He was socially conscience and spoke out against the plights of the poor.

After Meggyesy protested the anthem, he was benched. Even the anthem past is prologue.

* * *

"The main thing Kaepernick has accomplished is to inflame an engrossing debate and serve as a reminder that dissent is a form of patriotism, too," wrote columnist Sally Jenkins in September 2016 for the *Washington Post*.

Meanwhile, all Kaepernick did was, well, keep fighting. There's a quote he gave in 2016, toward the beginning of his fight. It remains one of his defining statements, and as some have tried to distort his message and what the movement was about, I always come back to these words. "I'll continue to sit," Kaepernick told reporters during one of his first press conferences, not long after his protest began. "I'm going to continue to stand with the people that are being oppressed. To me this is something that has to change. When there's significant change and I feel like that flag represents what it's supposed to represent, this country is representing people the way that it's supposed to, I'll stand."

Kaepernick stated repeatedly that, contrary to the repeated narrative, he wasn't protesting the military. "You can become a cop in six months," he said, "and you don't have to have the same amount of training as a cosmetologist. That's insane. I mean, someone that's holding a curling iron has more education and more training than people that have a gun and are going out on the street to protect us."

* * *

The erasure of Kaepernick became even more evident during Super Bowl LIV between the San Francisco 49ers and Kansas City Chiefs. The last time the 49ers made a Super Bowl was, of course, when

Kaepernick led them there after the 2012 season. Normally, a player like Kaepernick would have been a star during Super Bowl week; a carousel of player media appearances where the former player would have been a huge draw. Former 49ers quarterback Jeff Garcia and running back Frank Gore made constant visits on "Radio Row," but no Kaepernick. One league official privately confirmed that the league made no overtures for him to appear at the Super Bowl.

"They're trying to erase him," Houston Texans safety Michael Thomas told the *Wall Street Journal* in February 2020. "Even if you're not going to talk about the controversial part, at least talk about what he did on the field—which was electrifying."

In the playoffs leading up to the 49ers-Chiefs Super Bowl, 49ers running back Raheem Mostert broke Kaepernick's team playoff record for most rushing yards in a postseason game. Interestingly, the network didn't mention whose record Mostert had broken, something that is standard operating procedure in broadcast journalism (any journalism, for that matter). This, based on everything previously listed, was doubtfully an oversight. It seems in many corners of the NFL—or entities controlled or influenced by the league—are doing whatever they can to avoid mentioning his name.

And just in case there was any doubt that Kaepernick's name not being mentioned was a dramatic oversight, it wasn't mentioned, again, during the Super Bowl broadcast. This was an even larger scrub of history, since the last time the 49ers made the Super Bowl it was Kaepernick who was the quarterback.

That Super Bowl also demonstrated what was a slice of extraordinary hypocrisy. Whenever NFL players spoke about anything other than football, they were told by the league, and fans, to stick to sports. This wasn't the message solely to Kaepernick and the protesters. It was to all players. It's been that way for decades and has been especially so under the Trump administration.

The NFL, however, refused to stick to sports. It often interjected politics and propaganda . . . and this was especially true during the 49ers-Chiefs Super Bowl.

Wrote Dave Zirin of *The Nation*, "The reality of the Fox production of Super Bowl Sunday could be heard in a comment *Boston Globe* writer Ben Volin reported from a Fox executive: 'If it doesn't celebrate football or celebrate America, it's not going to be in the show.' The NFL's idea of 'celebrating football' was seen in a commercial where a young black child, with dyed blond hair, is seen running through a field of would-be tacklers, without helmets or pads, as NFL legends cheer him on. There was a shot of eighty-three-year-old legend Jim Brown sitting on a park bench telling him to 'take it to the house.' The child, in the middle of his epic jaunt, stopped in sad silence at a statue of the late NFL player turned Army Ranger Pat Tillman. This much-praised ad was football propaganda of the worst sort.

"As for celebrating 'America,'" Zirin continued, "this was seen by invoking militarism at every turn, even comparing NFL players to the troops. The only comparison, in the real world, is that both suffer from traumatic brain injuries that are covered up or scoffed at by their respective commanders in chief. The commercials also echoed this theme of one America, most grotesquely in an ad for Budweiser that celebrated the hugging of fully armored police by

a young black man at a standoff between riot cops and young protesters who were calling on police to stop killing them."

* * *

On January 8, 2018, Trump tweeted that "we are fighting for
our farmers, for our country, and for our GREAT AMERICAN
FLAG. We want our flag respected - and we want our NATIONAL
ANTHEM respected also!"

In a video of the president speaking to farmers, he mentioned
the anthem and flag, and how both should be cherished. "We're
fighting for our country and our great American flag. We are
fighting for our flag. We want our flag respected. We want our flag
respected, and we want our national anthem respected also." The
crowd composed of thousands gave Trump a standing ovation.

However, what's always been clear is that some people don't
practice what they preach. At almost every sporting event, all across
the country, large numbers of people don't respect the flag, or the
anthem. I've covered hundreds of NFL games, and in every one,
as the anthem played, people were eating, in line at the bathroom,
making out, drinking beer, texting, talking on their phones, or in
some cases, brawling.

Just under two years after Trump spoke about how the anthem
should be respected, he was holding a Super Bowl viewing party at
his Mar-a-Lago Club in Florida. The *Miami Herald* obtained video
of Trump laughing, dancing, and engaging with members as the
anthem played. On the video, Trump was barely paying attention
to the anthem at all.

Thus, in just about three years, the entire protest movement had come full circle. It began with the protest, then attacks from Trump lying about the intent of the protesters, saying they were making a mockery of the anthem. Then—and you cannot make this shit up—there's a video of Trump actually mocking the anthem.

Chapter 8

CHANGE

"The owners saw this as a fight, and just my opinion, but
I think many of them wanted to see Kaepernick destroyed."

—NFL general manager (who
requested to remain anonymous)

When Colin Kaepernick started the season on September 7,
2014, he and the 49ers were coming off three consecutive NFC
Championships, including one trip to the Super Bowl. It had been
a remarkable beginning to the Kaepernick and Jim Harbaugh era.
Things would soon change, however, as the 49ers began to crumble. After such success, it would be a slow and surprising fall.

But things didn't start out that way. That September game was
against the Dallas Cowboys, and the 49ers looked like the explosive group that had gone 36–11–1 over the past three seasons.
Kaepernick, with two touchdown passes to Vernon Davis, finished
the day with 201 yards passing and a 28–17 victory.

The following week, against the Chicago Bears, San Francisco
again started off hot, taking a commanding 20–7 lead into the

fourth quarter. Then came the issue that Kaepernick—and many young quarterbacks—face early in their careers: turnovers. In that game, he threw two interceptions and fumbled once, as the 49ers gave up 21 unanswered points in a 28–20 loss. While Kaepernick did not commit a turnover the following week against the Arizona Cardinals, his 49ers still lost, 23–14.

The team would win its next three games as Kaepernick stabilized his play. Looking back teammates remember how hard Kaep worked in the film room, and how that effort was even more pronounced after a loss. But there was something else happening at this time, too. This is when he became more vocal, opening up with the media about himself—specifically his thoughts on topics unrelated to football. When several reports emerged that he had a falling out with teammate Aldon Smith, who had been arrested for drunk driving and subsequently released, Kaepernick quickly and publicly disputed them.

"It's really tragic. And I wish him the best," Kaepernick said of Smith. "I hope he's doing well. I hope everything turns out alright for him and he gets back on track. I know this team misses his presence here. I was good friends with Aldon. He had just come to my golf tournament for Camp Taylor this past June to show support and help the kids."[1]

The site MediaTakeOut.com wrote that Smith crashed a car belonging to Kaepernick, noting the vehicle was his Mercedes. "Well, if I was a reporter, I would go about things logically,"

---

1 Smith was signed by the Dallas Cowboys in 2020 after being out of the NFL since 2015.

Kaepernick told the media in August 2015. "I would realize that I have a deal with Jaguar and have had it for a few years now, so I wouldn't be driving a Mercedes. I'd also realize we didn't have practice Thursday, so we weren't at the facility. Along those lines, anybody that believes that and goes about that reporting, just doesn't have the best integrity in my mind. To try to prey on athletes' livelihoods while one is going through a tough time is embarrassing to me. For people that do report that, put that out there and jumped on the bandwagon just to get Internet clicks and attention to their websites, it really is embarrassing that people do that."

A different public Kaepernick was clearly emerging. It just wasn't as stark and noticeable—yet.

* * *

In November 2015, after a 2–6 start to the season, the 49ers benched Kaepernick.

It was a moment few would have predicted just a few years earlier. Things reached a new low for him and the offense a month before, after a 20–3 loss to the divisional rival Seattle Seahawks. The 49ers punted nine times, had only eight first downs, and generated seven three-and-out drives. The 49ers had 142 total yards of offense—81 passing and 61 rushing—with six sacks allowed. It was the fourth time in the season that San Francisco had lost by 14 or more points.

Jim Harbaugh had since left for the University of Michigan, and though Harbaugh wasn't the most popular coach with segments of the locker room, his creativity, particularly when it came to building the offense around Kaepernick's talents, was superb.

His replacement, former assistant Jim Tomsula, was totally over-matched. He'd last just one season as head coach.

At a news conference following the Seahawks defeat, Tomsula expressed his frustration. "That game today was not what we want," Tomsula said. "It was not acceptable. We did not play well. We don't have an excuse. Again, that lies right here, and we need to do a better job. We're going to take the next few days and get after that."

Kaepernick was indeed struggling, but what was not gener-ally known was the physical toll his fearless and aggressive style of play was taking on his body. Mobile quarterbacks face a particular form of football violence; they take punishment while sitting in the pocket but also face hard hits when they leave it. Kaepernick was tall, fast, and physical, and defenses saw it as a challenge to take him on physically.

So it was likely only a matter of time before Kaepernick was seriously injured. That's what happened in October during a 17–3 loss to the Green Bay Packers. Kaepernick was doing some-thing he'd done many hundreds of times before—a read option handoff—when he has hit hard by linebacker Clay Matthews. Some weeks later, and about three weeks after he was benched, the team announced that Kaepernick was having surgery to repair a torn labrum in his left, nonthrowing shoulder. The rehab process would take him months to recover.

Playing hurt is a common occurrence for NFL players, but him appearing in four games after the injury was a testament to his durability. He was drafted in 2011, replaced Alex Smith during the 2012 season, and from that point had started 53 straight games before being injured. At that point, his 88.4 career passer rating was third in team history behind Steve Young (101.4) and Joe Montana (93.5). He added 1,832 regular-season yards and 11 passing touchdowns.

But Kaepernick would face more change; there'd later be operations on his thumb and a knee. After Tomsula was fired, Chip Kelly was hired in January 2016. Like Tomsula, Kelly would also last just one season before the franchise hired Kyle Shanahan in 2017.

It was during Kelly's tenure when Kaepernick began protesting. As a head coach, Kelly had been a disaster after leaving the University of Oregon. Nonetheless, something he said after his firing, later as an analyst for ESPN, was instructive. The narrative then (which is still wrongly stated as fact) is that the protests by Kaepernick and Reid were disruptive and a distraction to the team. Kelly said that wasn't accurate, per an interview on Adam Schefter's podcast in 2017:

> We heard from the outside about what a distraction it is. Except those people aren't in our locker room, and it never was a distraction. And Kaep never brought that and never turned it into a circus . . . came to work every day, extremely diligent in terms of his preparation, in terms of his work ethic in the weight room, in terms of his work ethic in the meeting room, and I really enjoyed Kaep. I've talked to Kaep three or four times since we both left San Francisco. I know he's working out really hard in New York right now, and I think he's a really good person and a really good player, and I really enjoyed coaching him. . . . when you're not there, it's easy to speculate on what it's like, but he is zero distraction.

Another change Kaepernick faced was resistance from people who didn't agree with his protests. After President Trump's open ridicule of Kaepernick and those protesting, the conservative media jumped on the bandwagon, attacking them with thorny viciousness.

In September 2017, Fox News host Laura Ingraham took aim at the protesting NFL players. "Part of me is like, a lot of these guys are punks," she said on her radio show. "I mean, that's part of me, like, that's the old-fashioned Connecticut Yankee in me. It's like, you've got to be kidding me, you guys are like—you guys are the elite of the elite. You make millions of dollars to play a game, you're like—can't stand for the national anthem? You've got to be kidding me."

In addition, Fox News' Sean Hannity, who has four million Twitter followers and three million viewers on television, said on his television show, after Nike released a groundbreaking ad featuring Kaepernick, "There are plenty of heroes in this country that Nike could feature, but [a] Castro-loving . . . cop-hating, ex-three-year-backup quarterback is not one of them."

"In the United States of America," right-wing commentator Tomi Lahren said in December 2017, "we say the Pledge of Allegiance, we recite the Declaration of Independence, and we sure as hell sing the 'Star Bangled Banner' before sporting events. If you don't like it, get the hell out. Go salute another flag or recite the Quran in one of those other countries you like so much." Lahren's right-wing counterpart, Jason Whitlock, said on Fox that Kaepernick "doesn't want to be a football player, he wants to be a social justice warrior and move to Hollywood."

Conservative commentator Ben Shapiro said in 2017 that Kaepernick is "championed as this thought leader, even though I'm not sure Colin Kaepernick has ever had any real thought." Radio host

Michael Savage, who has approximately eleven million listeners a week, told his audience: "That boy needs to stick to throwing a ball. He should stand up and respect the flag, like other patriotic Americans." Savage knew, of course, what he was doing by calling an African American man "boy."

The slow and steady creep of ring-wing extremism into the NFL media culture had many repercussions but one in particular. Despite a number of players participating in the protests, the venom still had a chilling effect. Some players saw how Kaepernick and other protesters were treated and, understandably, wanted no part of it. The average career of an NFL player is around three years. They don't have guaranteed contracts. They are actually, in many ways, the most vulnerable of the big four professional sports. The players know this and, most important, the owners do too.

* * *

Finally, the other change Kaepernick faced was physical. He was losing weight, dropping almost 20 pounds due to his numerous injuries. It was becoming clear that Kaep didn't want to stay with the 49ers, and the 49ers didn't want him. This notion was starting to leak into the media. "Regardless of politics or not, he has a very, very big uphill battle to make this team," Fox Sports' Jay Glazer said during one Fox radio broadcast in 2017. "I'd be shocked if he's on the 49ers by the time this season [2017] ends. It has nothing to do with political views whatsoever. He lost a ton of weight this offseason, had three surgeries, couldn't work out, lost that double threat, that size-speed ratio. No political views, he just hasn't been effective. He's regressing as a player. I'd be shocked if he's on this roster by the end of this year. He may not be on it in the next two weeks."

In 2016, as the protests began, Kaepernick spent extensive time at his locker explaining his rationale to the numerous media inquiries. This is when I first met him, and it was one of the more emotional and powerful series of moments I've ever experienced. He was strong and certain. More than anything—particularly since I understood the inner workings of the league—it was clear he was likely sacrificing his career for his beliefs. Because of this, he was one of the most noble people I'd encountered in my twenty-five years of covering the game.

But it wasn't just me; Kaepernick had this effect on many people. For all those who said they hated him, there was a legion of others who adored him. Symone Sanders, the former press secretary for senator Bernie Sanders and later senior adviser to vice president Joe Biden's presidential campaign, attended a September 2017 rally supporting the quarterback, which took place outside the Manhattan offices of the NFL. "He's out there kneeling for my son and your son and my daughter," Sanders remembered in an interview with the *Washington Post*. "The crowd was just overtaken with emotion at that moment, and everybody understood that this was absolutely bigger than Colin Kaepernick."

"One day, maybe my youngest, who is in second grade, is going to open up a history book and he'll read about Colin," said Phil Sanchez, Kaepernick's former high school guidance counselor, also to the *Washington Post*. "And it won't have anything to do with throwing a touchdown."

Again, what people most admired was Colin's bravery and honesty, and there was plenty of bluntness.

"We are under attack! It's clear as day!" Kaepernick wrote a day later, alongside a video showing the immediate aftermath of the death of Philando Castile, who was shot five times in his car by a Minnesota police officer, with his girlfriend and her four-year-old daughter in the vehicle.

"I couldn't see another #SandraBland, #TamirRice, #WalterScott, #EricGarner," Kaepernick told reporters in the summer of 2017. "The list goes on and on and on. At what point do we do something about it?"

Chapter 9

ALLIES

"With what's going on, I'd rather see him take a knee than stand up, put his hands up, and get murdered, so, my take on it is, shit's gotta start somewhere, and if that was the starting point, I just hope people open up their eyes and see there's really a problem going on and something needs to be done for it to stop. And if you're really not racist, then you won't see what he's doing as a threat to America but just addressing a problem we have."

—Marshawn Lynch, Oakland Raiders running back, on *Conan*, September 20, 2016

On January 5, 2014, the game-time temperature at Lambeau Field was a frigid 5 degrees Fahrenheit. It was, at the time, the seventh-coldest game in NFL history. Most players were covered with cold weather gear, yet Colin Kaepernick was sleeveless. The message he was sending was clear: fuck the weather.

"It's not that cold," Kaepernick told a television reporter. "It's all mental."

The San Francisco 49ers would beat the Green Bay Packers in this Wild Card Round but what happened was bigger than that.

What's often lost with Kaepernick's career is how mentally strong he was. This strength would manifest itself in different ways once he began protesting. But on this January day in Wisconsin, it was strictly channeled into football. And in many moments, just like this one, Kaepernick was difficult to stop. No matter how much the 49ers fell behind, the team always felt their quarterback gave them a chance.

Kaepernick saved the 49ers on multiple occasions on this day, on key runs which helped set up scores. Twice the Packers took the lead from the 49ers—once in the second quarter and then again in the fourth—and in both instances Kaepernick responded with scrambles that kept his team's drives alive. One run went for 42 yards to help put the Niners back in front, 13–7, in the second quarter. Then, and after they fell behind, 17–13, he bolted 24 yards to set up another score, giving the 49ers a 20–17 lead. When the Packers tied the score at 20 late in the fourth, Kaepernick rescued the 49ers again.

On 3rd-and-8 from the Green Bay 38-yard line, just outside field goal range with 1:10 left on the clock, Kaepernick rolled left to get away from the pass rush, then ran 11 yards to keep the drive alive and move the ball into field goal range. The kick was made by Phil Dawson and the 49ers moved on with a 23–20 victory. Kaepernick finished the day with 227 yards, one touchdown and one interception. He also ran the ball seven times for 98 yards. It's that latter number which made him so dangerous, and essentially won the game for San Francisco.

The win was the 49ers' seventh in a row, but equally as impressive was it being Kaepernick's fourth-straight victory over the

Packers dating back to 2012. Few players at that time, and perhaps ever, had dominated the Packers the way Kaepernick did.

"Colin Kaepernick," Harbaugh said after the game, "I think we can all agree, is a clutch performer."

* * *

What few knew at the time was that as Kaepernick was excelling as a quarterback and becoming one of the league's true stars, he was also closely watching what was happening across American society.

What athletes would eventually face was a more militarized conservative America that was intolerant of protest—or, well, intolerant of protest from black men. "The 2012 killing of Trayvon Martin and the 2014 Ferguson unrest in the wake of Michael Brown's killing," wrote Howard Bryant in his book *Heritage*, "followed by several high-profile killings of African Americans by police, brought the players, led by LeBron James, out from behind the tinted glass of their Escalades." What Kaepernick did with his protest, indirectly, was not just wake athletes up but also force them to examine their role in this fight. "I'm in support of anybody who has convictions to believe in something and willing to pay the price and take the lumps and take the hits and the backlash that's coming from it," said former Baltimore Ravens and New York Jets linebacker Bart Scott, now an analyst for CBS, during one broadcast.

"One of Colin's messages to athletes," said Kenny Stills to me, "is that the money we make, or the power we have, won't necessarily protect us. If we are stopped by an officer who has hate in his heart, we could suffer too."

* * *

Quarterback Cam Newton remembers the game his Carolina Panthers played against the 49ers on January 12, 2014.

"I'd seen him play before that game, and I was always amazed by everything he could do," said Newton. "I think there were a lot of quarterbacks who played the way I did, who saw Colin as model for how to play the game. What he did in that game was what he always did. He played hard and smart."

After the contest, Kaepernick and Newton embraced near midfield. It was an important moment as there had rarely been two starting African American quarterbacks in the postseason. In fact, there have been just seven total instances where two black quarterbacks met in the divisional round, and two instances in the conference championships. It was also important because the 49ers were heading to their third consecutive NFC title game.

However, as the game unfolded, it did not seem like it would turn out that way. It didn't always seem like it would go that way. Kaepernick struggled early, going only 11-for-24, while Newton gave Carolina the lead with a 31-yard touchdown to wide receiver Steve Smith in the second quarter. The Panthers held the 49ers to just 59 total yards with only several minutes remaining in the first half. That's when Kaepernick started to Kaepernick.

He led the 49ers on a 12-play, 80-yard touchdown drive that gave San Francisco a 13–10 lead with five seconds left in the first half. They'd never trail again. Kaepernick had only 196 passing yards, but as he'd done so many times before, he impacted the game in other ways. In one of the final San Francisco drives of the game—and the most important—Kaepernick led the offense 77 yards in eight plays. The drive ended with Kaepernick scampering 4 yards for a touchdown, putting the 49ers up, 20–10.

Years later, in 2018, as Newton was preparing to play a 49ers team without Kaepernick (he still wasn't on a team), Newton went off script with the media and suddenly began discussing Kaepernick's plight. Until that point, Newton hadn't discussed Kaepernick. In fact, he'd been cautious about wading into any issues that didn't deal with football. But Newton felt he needed to address what was the effective banning of a quarterback he highly respected.

"I think it's unfair," Newton said of Kaepernick not being in the league. "In my opinion do I think Kaepernick is better than some of these starting quarterbacks in this league? Absolutely. Should he be on a roster? In my opinion, absolutely, there's no question about it. Is he good enough to be on a roster? Is he good enough to be a starting quarterback? Absolutely."

At that point, in fact, Kaepernick had more road playoff wins than all other 49ers quarterbacks combined. Hall of Famers Joe Montana and Steve Young went a combined 1-6 in road playoff games.

Kaepernick would again face his nemesis, the Seahawks, who often frustrated the quarterback. Yet, off the field, there were few teams who backed the movement with more fervor, and dedication, than Seattle.

* * *

The Seahawks that Kaepernick would play in the NFC title game on January 19th, 2014, were a lot like Kaepernick. At the time both were in a sort of embryonic stage. Their attitudes about the league they played in, and the men who ran it, particularly Commissioner Roger Goodell and the owners, were being formed. Kaepernick's 49ers and the Seahawks would become fierce rivals and engage in some of the most heated battles in recent playoff history. Yet off the field it was different. Years after the 2014 title game, as Kaepernick began protesting, members of the Seahawks would become some of his biggest allies.

Before we get to that game, we need to take a look at who the Seahawks are, and how they became one of the most powerful forces during the protest movement.

The Seahawks were a highly intelligent, fiery group. They were a blend of footballers and activists who loved the sport but were also going to fight to make it better, in every incarnation of that phrase. An *ESPN: The Magazine* story headline, from May 2017, said a great deal about how they approached football: "Why Richard Sherman Can't Let Go of Seattle's Super Bowl Loss." Just a few months after the Seattle Seahawks continued to transform the NFL with a bullying, swashbuckling, and talkative team that feared no one, or any franchise, they were back at practice. Their season was a success but they'd still lost to the New England Patriots on the last play of the Super Bowl. That moment had left a bitter taste and a strong desire, especially from the defensive players, to avenge that loss with a return trip to the championship game. To some of the players that meant get tougher, nastier, and more relentless than ever before. That's where Sherman came in. That's where Sherman always came in.

Fights had broken out all practice. No one cared. That was the Seahawk way. "Iron forges iron" is how the Seahawks put it. What happened next, however, had never occurred before. Quarterback Russell Wilson threw an interception to Sherman. Sherman, who liked to play head games with quarterbacks, even his own, became incensed. Sherman took the football and threw it back at Wilson. The ball skipped in front of Wilson, near his feet.

"You fucking suck!" Sherman yelled at Wilson.

Fights again broke out between the offense and defense, as the ESPN story noted. The defensive players were laughing; Wilson and some on the offense were not. The divide that always separated the two entities was now no longer a cold war. It was a full-blown battle.

It was in these moments where the Seahawks were created, and it was in these moments they became an almost unbeatable force with heroes like Michael Bennett and Sherman who would take on football on and off the field. They were some of the original fearless fighters of this NFL era.

The fighting at practice, and the fearless nature of that group overall, was key during the battles of the players against the league, and then Trump. When the president would attack, Seahawks players were often first to respond. They refused to back down even to Trump.

There were two truths about the Seahawks: first, they operated like a team from the 1970s, where grievances and beefs were worked out mostly between the players in the locker room. The Seahawks were old school in a time of gloss and high-tech twenty-first-century football. Second, they were just good. Really good. As good as the league has ever seen, standing alongside such great organizations as the Patriots, Packers, and Steelers. That talent, and their winning, was one of the things that gave them credibility when they were among the teams vocally backing Kaepernick and taking on Trump.

Bennett, the smart and politically savvy former defensive end for the Seahawks, once joked that playing for them was like playing on top of a hot stove. "We put the fire to each other," he told me during an interview in 2018. "You either survived all of that pressure or you folded. That pressure made us better. No one shied from it. I wanted it. There were no conformers. No lazy players. We all spit fire because we were made from fire."

"We were so tough to each other that nothing scared us," he told me. "Politics didn't scare us. The president didn't scare us. Roger Goodell certainly didn't scare us. We were all a bunch of fighters."

As Seattle's confidence and power grew, as well as the team's outspokenness, behind the scenes the league office wanted to find ways to make peace with the Seahawks players. Many of them had come to not just openly criticize Goodell and the NFL but mock them as dickless men incapable of understanding what it was really like to play in the NFL. The culmination of this fight came when the Seahawks reached the Super Bowl and Marshawn Lynch refused to cooperate with media-day festivities. He told reporters "I'm here so I don't get fined" in response to any media query. Though most readers will remember this, what they don't know is what happened privately before and after that moment. The NFL attempted to broker a number of private meetings between the Seahawks and NFL brass in New York, but the players, several of them explained, rebuffed the league. That was also the Seahawks way. They had no interest in making peace with Goodell, whom they viewed as an oppressive entity.

They were one of the few teams that saw the NFL for what it was—a system that made players wealthy but also restricted their freedoms and expression. The Seahawks weren't the first to battle the NFL patriarchy. As previously mentioned, Cleveland running back Jim Brown had taken on the NFL's pay structure and its lack of desire (if not downright hostility) to enter into the civil rights battles of the 1960s. Decades later, Kaepernick's heartfelt and brave peaceful protests would again challenge the NFL's power structure. Bracketed between Brown and Kaepernick were almost no NFL cultural warriors except the Seahawks.

Both Kaepernick and the Seahawks came to believe the player base had become too placated by money and were forgetting how to use their power to fight for something bigger than football. The Seahawks reminded the NFL that players had power and should use it. The brother of Michael Bennett, Martellus, who spent nine years in the NFL, once said, "A black man using his voice is the most dangerous thing in the NFL. They can tolerate anything else for the most part, but once you start speaking out on anything, it's over."

The power of the Seahawks went far beyond their Super Bowl appearances and what they did on the field, although those were singularly remarkable feats. Parts of the Seattle locker room publicly backed the Black Lives Matter movement. That movement, and the player protests, became heavily intertwined. The Seahawks joined and embraced their roles as counteragents.

It was the Seattle players that forged paths for socially conscious teams like the NBA's Golden State Warriors. They caught the attention of presidents and world leaders. In cities like Baltimore and Kansas City, players were despised for their protests during the national anthem, often booed by fans. In Seattle, it was different. The protests were cherished.

As players were continuing to kneel in support of Kaepernick, the president continued to notice. "Wouldn't you love to see one of these NFL owners, when somebody disrespects our flag, to say, 'Get that son of a bitch off the field right now. Out! He's fired. He's fired!'" Trump said at the 2017 rally in Alabama. He added: "You know, some owner is going to do that. He's going to say, 'That guy that disrespects our flag, he's fired.' And that owner, they don't know it [but] they'll be the most popular person in this country. . . . When people like yourselves turn on television and you see those people taking the knee when they're playing our great national anthem. The only thing you could do better is if you see it, even if it's one player, leave the stadium."

* * *

Meanwhile, Trump was having private conversations with several NFL owners, including Dallas' Jerry Jones, and the Patriots' Robert Kraft, about the protesting players. Trump, according to a variety of sources, was hoping NFL owners would indeed do exactly as he ranted at that rally—fire NFL players for peacefully protesting. Trump also asked several owners to make such a firing a spectacle by holding a press conference and giving Trump credit for the cutting of the player.

The umbilical cord between Trump and many NFL owners was straight and tight. Most of them not only agreed with the president's views that the protests were wrong but also actually *liked* him. There were a handful that didn't, but most backed him. Some, like Jones, perhaps the most powerful of all owners across all American sports, did so publicly. Owners in other sports, however, had different views. One year before Kaepernick began his protests, a twenty-five-year-old man named Freddie Gray, from Baltimore, died while in police custody. A medical examiner ruled that Gray's death was a homicide due to the officers not taking steps to save his life after they physically attacked him. His death would later be one of the sparks for Kaepernick. But before his response, Baltimore had already erupted in protest. It wasn't just the Gray case, it was what his death represented, which was a decades-long series of police abuses and harassment of Baltimore's black community.

However, unlike many owners, who walked lockstep with Trump, the Orioles' executive vice president, John Angelos, made it clear his team stood independently. Angelos additionally did something few other owners in any sport did in response to the president. Angelos spoke with affection, and also with deep sympathy, about the plight of the black community, in this case the community in Baltimore: "My greater source of personal concern, outrage and sympathy beyond this particular case is focused neither upon one night's property damage nor upon the acts," wrote Angelos in a statement, "but it is focused rather upon the past four-decade period during which an American political elite have shipped middle class jobs away from Baltimore and cities and towns around the U.S. to third-world dictatorships like China and others. Plunged tens of millions of good, hard working Americans into economic devastation, and then followed that action around the nation by diminishing every American's civil rights protections in order to control an unfairly impoverished population living under an ever-declining standard of living and suffering at the butt end of an ever-more militarized and aggressive surveillance state."

To this day, Angelos's statement remains the marker, the thing all owners should aspire to reach. No NFL owner, then or since, has said anything even remotely as empathetic as Angelos's words.

An important thing to remember about this time is that words like Angelos's—thoughtful and kind—were counterbalanced by a right-wing media that, well, didn't show that type of class. The resistance the movement faced didn't just come from Trump. It came from the entirety of the right's media ecosystem.

* * *

In a September 2016 piece by Olivia Dupree, titled "Analysis: How the Right and Left-Wing Media Have Covered the Kaepernick Scandal," she compiled the clips below. They are a small window into how the right-wing media often spoke about Kaepernick.

"Colin, I support your right to freedom of speech and expression," said conservative commentator Tomi Lahren. "It's this country, the country that you have so much disdain for that allows you the right to speak your mind. It protects your right to be a whiny, indulgent, attention-seeking crybaby, and it protects my right to shred you for it."

"Next time Kaepernick wants to talk about social issues, maybe he can find a more respectful way to do it that does not make him look like a disrespectful tool," wrote Red State contributor Kyle Foley.

"Maybe he should find a country that works better for him," said Trump at a rally. "Let him try. It won't happen."

Ben Shapiro, editor-in-chief of the conservative podcast the Daily Wire, said that Kaepernick "represents the mainstream left. If you say, 'I don't think America is a very racist place. I think America is a great place,' then you get ripped as a sellout. You get ripped as an Uncle Tom. If you do what Kaepernick did, you get praised by the media: sports and political both."

Stated longtime radio extremist Rush Limbaugh, recently awarded the Presidential Medal of Freedom from Trump, "I've warned of the politicization of everything. There now doesn't seem to be a single aspect of life in the United States that is not touched, that does not become controversial because of race. Thank you, President Obama. Even the national anthem has now become a matter of race."

Radio host Mark Levin said of Kaepernick via *Breitbart* in August 2016, "Because a dimwit with a 12 IQ, like this guy, can make $126 million in six years based on one or two seasons, and he still sucks. When he doesn't stand during the national anthem it's not because of social injustice or anything else. He's spitting on the men and women who are in one hell-hole all over this country fighting for that flag, fighting for this nation, and every one of them that came before them—every one of them. That's why this is important—not because of him. He's unimportant. Not because of one principal who says you can't bring in the American flag. You might offend an ethnic group. Because this is going on everywhere."

"I don't want you to stand," Levin said. "I don't want you to stand. You stay seated. You're not allowed to stand. You stay seated, you jerk. You stay seated. That's how you'll honor this country—by getting out of the way and staying out of the way. You're an insignificant fly. That's right, I said it!"

"I watched Colin Kaepernick, and I thought it was terrible, and then it got bigger and bigger and started mushrooming, and frankly the NFL should have suspended him for one game, and he would have never done it again," Trump told Fox News' Sean Hannity in a 2018 interview. "They could have then suspended him for two games, and they could have suspended him if he did it a third time, for the season, and you would never have had a problem. But I will tell you, you cannot disrespect our country, our flag, our anthem—you cannot do that."

The message was clear. It wasn't just that Kaepernick was a convenient target for conservatives and Trump. He was more than that to them. He was a means to an end. He was an avatar used to remind people that black and brown people weren't just growing in power—a black had become president, for God's sake—they were becoming more willing to disrupt the country's power centers. And, yes, football was a power center. Every year, NFL games are among the most-watched shows on television. In 2018–2019, NFL Sunday Night Football, NFL Monday Night Football, and NFL Thursday Night Football were among the top five watched shows.

Only *Game of Thrones* beat football.

* * *

Across the league, every player noticed Trump's ugly verbiage, and no antennas were higher than those in Seattle. Players were incensed over Trump targeting the league. One postpractice, as players were changing and getting dressed, there was one of several makeshift Trump-bashing sessions. As Trump's attacks became more numerous and acidic the anger among some Seattle players increased.

Seahawks players, in response to Trump, began reaching out to other teams. Informal conversations became plans of attacks. One thing that all players decided: they would not allow Trump to intimidate them or shut them up. They would speak out whenever asked about Trump by the media. Such a move was actually a bold step. Almost every team in the NFL was telling its players to avoid discussing Trump, and initially, some did. But players on teams like the Seahawks, Eagles, Ravens, and Dolphins refused to be quiet in face of the bigoted words from Trump.

Never before in the history of the NFL had a group of players united so closely, and publicly, against the president. It was always the opposite. The NFL had long been the most militaristic of all the professional sports, and the most supportive of Republican administrations.

The Seahawks started responding in earnest to Trump publicly in 2017 following the enactment of a new NFL rule. In an attempt to strangle the player protests—without appearing to do so—Commissioner Roger Goodell implemented a policy mandating that players on the sideline stand during the anthem. Protesting players, the new rule stated, had to remain in the locker room during the anthem.

Trump wasn't satisfied and suggested that any protesting NFL player—whether in the locker room or on the sideline—should be deported. This incensed the Seahawks. "He's an idiot. Plain and simple," receiver Doug Baldwin said. "Listen, I respect the man because he's a human being, first and foremost. But he's just being more divisive, which is not surprising. It is what it is. For him to say that anybody who doesn't follow his viewpoints or his constituents' viewpoints should be kicked out of the country, it's not very empathetic, it's not very American-like, actually, to me. It's not very patriotic. It's not what this country was founded upon. It's kind of ironic to me that the president of the United States is contradicting what our country is really built on."

* * *

It's important to remember Kaepernick, protesting players, and the Seahawks weren't just fighting Trump, or right-wing media, but the NFL itself. Particularly, NFL ownership. Most NFL owners have long viewed players as drones that are easily replaced. Players fought against this in a variety of ways, some of them unique, and Seattle and Oakland running back Marshawn Lynch was certainly that. A typical Marshawn Lynch moment happened in Oakland and he proved, yet again, Lynch has no fucks to give. It remains one of the things that makes him fascinating and a cult hero.

Lynch is a mix of superhuman ability, mental strength, smarts, and brutality. He was raised by a formidable and kind mother who used to give Lynch the candy Skittles in the minutes before Lynch's high school games to calm him.

Lynch has been one of the most charitable men in the league. In 2018, he was named the Raiders' Walter Payton Man of the Year, mostly due to his Fam1st Family Foundation, dedicated to helping underprivileged youth in the Oakland area.

Yet it hasn't all been smooth for Lynch. He had his license revoked in 2008 while playing for Buffalo after he hit a twenty-seven-year-old woman with his car and didn't stop. There was a gun charge and a DUI allegation as well. But after arriving in Seattle there was no trouble, and he's become as big a cult hero as has ever played in the NFL.

The Seahawks are among the most noteworthy entities in this time of fearless fighters, because so many of the strong personalities on the team, in all of their independence, creativity, and smarts, combined into a forceful resistance to Trump.

Not to mention they were excellent football players. Just ask quarterback Peyton Manning. One thing he remembers about playing the Seahawks in Super Bowl XLVIII is the relentlessness of the defense. "Once we fell behind, they jumped on us," Manning said, "and they never stopped." Manning added, "That was one of the most vicious defenses I ever faced."

It's difficult to put into words how impressive the Seahawks were in that game. Manning's offense at the time was the best in football. The Broncos were destroying teams with a passing game that seemed unstoppable. The Seahawks stuffed Manning, jumped to a 15–0 lead, then intercepted him and scored on a 69-yard return. The 43–8 Seahawks victory was one of the most dominant in Super Bowl history.

At a time when the NFL, like now, was a passing league, the Seahawks went retrograde. It remains one of the more remarkable parts of how they rose to dominance. In the same way the team drafted players that other franchises rejected, and hired a coach in Pete Carroll who had twice been fired, it's fitting the Seahawks crafted a team that bucked the trend of where football was offensively by focusing on the running game and defense. It was that way in the opening game, in September 2013, when they bashed the Carolina Panthers and won a low-scoring game, 12–7. Or when they bullied the 49ers, 29–3, in the following game. By Week 3 of that season the Seahawks were allowing the fewest points in the league. Against Houston, one week after that, Sherman scored on a 58-yard interception return.

After winning the Super Bowl, the Seahawks made a visit to the White House where the occupant actually liked them. Barack Obama, during a celebration of their Super Bowl win, and with the entire Seahawks team standing behind him, started the proceedings with a joke.

"Let's give it up for this quiet, reserved bunch called the Seattle Seahawks," said President Barak Obama. "World champions. Best football team in America."

The mayor of Seattle was there. There were members of Congress who were Seahawks fans there. Another Seahawks fan, Sally Jewell, the Secretary of the Interior, who was born in London but grew up in Washington State, was there. The heart of Obama's speech focused on one of the core ingredients of those Seahawks: their outspokenness. Even the POTUS, the man who heads the most powerful nation on Earth and with much bigger fish to fry, knew the Seahawks were big talkers. Their legend of the Seahawks wasn't just an NFL thing. Or a Seattle thing. Or even a state of Washington thing. Their essence had drawn the attention of a president.

"We are here to celebrate," Obama said, "the first Super Bowl victory for the city of Seattle. . . . Of course I don't need to tell you how outstanding the Seahawks are," Obama joked, "because they did a pretty good job of describing themselves as outstanding during the year."

And in typical Lynch fashion, he didn't show up. President Obama didn't skip a beat. "I am sorry that Marshawn's not here," he said. "I just wanted to say how much I admire his approach to the press. I wanted to get some tips from him." As everyone laughed, someone in the crowd yelled out one of Lynch's favorite phases. "'Bout that action," someone remarked.

"It's about that action." Obama said.

The most poignant moment came when Obama turned to Russell Wilson. It was the first African American president speaking to only the second African American quarterback to ever win a Super Bowl. "The best part about it is, no one commented on it," Obama said during the team's 2014 visit to the White House, "which tells you the progress that we've made, although we have more progress to make."

"So let me just say that as a guy who was elected president with the name Barak Obama, I root for the underdogs."

* * *

But before all of that, before a visit with Obama, and before the movement began, came one of the defining games for both Seattle and Kaepernick. In many ways, the 2014 title game against Seattle was the start of Kaepernick's exit from the NFL, and on his way out, he'd face one of the toughest defenses the league has ever seen. "We really respected what Colin could do," remembers Richard Sherman. "But we had so many fast guys on defense who could run with him, and we could blanket his receivers."

For one of the few times in his career, Kaepernick would face a defense as fast and as athletic as he was. The Seahawks possessed the top-ranked defense in football, allowing only 273.6 yards a game and 231 total points for the year, and the team had 39 take-aways, all league highs. In many ways, Kaepernick and the 49ers didn't stand a chance, yet there they were hanging with Seattle, until the last few seconds of the game.

Trailing 23–17 the 49ers got the football back one last time with 3:32 left in the contest. Kaepernick completed four con-secutive passes, including a dart to Frank Gore on fourth down, which put San Francisco at the Seattle 18-yard line.

Kaepernick threw a high pass to wide receiver Michael Crabtree yet Sherman, guarding Crabtree, got a piece of the football, and the football landed in the hands of linebacker Malcolm Smith. Game over. All Seattle had to do was run out the clock.

There was a moment after that's discussed to this day. Sherman spoke to Fox sideline reporter Erin Andrews, and in one powerful interview, Sherman's words symbolized both his status as a strong personality, and the Seahawks as a cultural phenomenon.

"Well I'm the best corner in the game. When you try me with a sorry receiver like (Michael) Crabtree that's the result you're going to get," Sherman told Andrews, yelling. "Don't you ever talk about me." When Andrews asked him who was talking about him, Sherman said "*Crabtree*" before continuing. "Don't you open your mouth about the best. Or I'm gonna shut it for you real quick. LOB." LOB as in "Legion of Boom," the nickname for Seahawks secondary.

The interview, frankly, was amazing. Most of all, it was some-thing different from most television postgame interviews in that it was substantive and entertaining. In the hours and days after it, Sherman was called a thug by more conservative viewers, and his words were called a "wild rant" in a CBSSports.com head-line. Nonconservative viewers saw Sherman as a star. Like other Seahawks players, he challenged many people's ideas of what it means to be a football player in the twenty-first century. Sherman was everything a football player was supposed to be. He knew it and didn't care if you understood that or not. Many Seahawks players felt the same way.

"I think all Richard was doing was reminding the NFL how good he was," said Andrews. "He was also letting the world know that the Seahawks were not to be underestimated."

The 49ers and Seahawks became hardened rivals but also appreciative of each other from afar. There was a kinship that went beyond what happened on the field, and this connection, built up over years, was crucial when Kaepernick began protesting.

Chapter 10

MR. ROGER'S NEIGHBORHOOD

"Those who cannot remember the past are condemned to repeat it."

—George Santayana

Being the leader of the most popular sports league isn't easy. Commissioner Roger Goodell answers to the owners—they pay his salary—while simultaneously disciplining them. He is the players' boss, while also trying to be their friend. He is a conduit to the fans despite so many of them despising him. Goodell is paid handsomely (he earned $31.5 million in 2015—the last year his salary was reported), so all of that cash is a perfect armor for the legions of fans who despise him.

Some of the hatred is unfair, but much of it is deserved. He has mishandled everything from player sexual misconduct to the deflating of footballs. The handling of the Ray Rice case, where he was caught on video punching his fiancé and knocking her unconscious, was so botched the NFL had to hire a special investigator to examine the league's handling of the video. That investigator's name was Robert Mueller.

Perhaps what Goodell has mishandled the most was the situation of players kneeling. Goodell, appealing to the conservative portion of his fanbase—and a mostly conservative ownership—rebuked the face of the protests, Colin Kaepernick. Then they mostly ignored him. Because there was no cogent strategy on how to deal with the protests, the media—some of it hostile—initially set the message as the NFL stayed quiet. This allowed the issue to grow in the NFL, and as Kaepernick was clearly blackballed by the league, it deepened the resentment of the player base. It was only a matter of time before the players erupted—and they did. The players long had issues with Goodell, but how Kaepernick was treated really exposed that rift.

Before the anthem protests evolved into one of the bigger sports stories in recent history, a small group of high-profile players decided to write Goodell and Troy Vincent, the NFL's executive vice president in charge of football operations. The purpose of the letter was simple: it was an action plan on how NFL players could fight for social justice.

"To be clear, we are asking for your support," the letter began. "We appreciate your acknowledgment on the call regarding the clear distinction between support and permission. For us, support means: bear all or part of the weight of; hold up; give assistance to, especially financially; enable to function or act. We need support, collaboration and partnerships to achieve our goal of strengthening the community."

* * *

"There is one thing that you really need to know about Roger," says someone close to him, who has worked with Goodell for years. "He is immensely transactional."

The most important man in this entire story is Colin Kaepernick, who was the face of the movement. The second is President Donald Trump, who used the movement to stoke racism and division among Americans. The third is commissioner Roger Goodell, because he is the most important man in the NFL.

He is essentially the voice of ownership. He's their avatar, and how he handles his responsibilities is vastly different from his predecessors.

Pete Rozelle is considered one of the most highly regarded commissioners in league history. Publicly, he had an image as a consensus builder. But that wasn't always the case. He strong-armed owners and built consensus through manipulation and deceit.

Another former commissioner, Paul Tagliabue, was also different from Goodell. For one, he had no issue telling the owners to screw off. He was also immensely trusted by the upper echelon of the players union. Tagliabue built a coalition with the players—sometimes over the objections of the owners, many of whom believed the best way to deal with players was with force and intimidation.

On important difference from his predecessors is Goodell's consistent compliance with the wishes of team owners. He also joined with ownership in the belief that growing revenues, above all else, was the mission. Tagliabue was, in fact, so disturbed by Goodell's constant chase of money over all else that he criticized him in a 2015 article for *GQ* magazine that profiled Goodell, saying, "If [players] see you making decisions only in economic terms, they start to understand that and question what you're all about. There's a huge intangible value in peace. There's a huge intangible value in having allies."

* * *

This backdrop is vital because it explains why the NFL, almost immediately, objected on a cellular level to Kaepernick's protest. Goodell couldn't take Kaepernick's side the way, perhaps, the NBA commissioner Adam Silver would, because Goodell was a representative of the owners, and the majority of owners disliked what Kaepernick was doing, were afraid of the financial impact, or had some combination of the two. It's true that, to some degree, every NFL commissioner represents the owners, but none like Goodell. Rozelle ran the owners, Tagliabue manipulated or ignored them, but Goodell has served them.

It was easy to see the difference between the approaches of Goodell and Silver in something the NBA commissioner told NBC's Craig Melvin in 2019. Silver was defending NBA players who refused the traditional postchampionship visit to the White House. "If done respectfully and if a player chooses to say, 'I don't support that president or particular policies of that president' that makes the player, hopefully, like every other American," Silver said. "What I've said about people who have said to me, 'How can you let a player criticize the president?' I've always said, 'This is America.'"

As for Roger Goodell, he looked across the league—and the large ballrooms where owners and league officials gathered several times a year—and saw a simple number: twenty-four of thirty-two.

* * *

In the end, Goodell's management style exacerbated the tensions during the protests. Whereas Rozelle bullied owners to get his way, and Tagliabue often ignored them and got things done by treating players as allies, Goodell did something more self-preserving. "Most of all," the former NFL executive explained, "Roger was a vote-counter. He read the room and saw what the room was telling him."

What the room, what the owners were telling Goodell to was squash the protests, and eventually, that's exactly what happened.

Many of the owners were also woefully out of touch with the modern athlete—or, actually, anything modern. There were owners who until just several years ago were still using flip phones. Former Carolina Panthers owner Jerry Richardson didn't know how to retrieve his voicemail. The idea that most NFL owners could grapple with the complexities of race relations in the era of Trump (or in general)—even if they wanted to—was ludicrous. They had no clue and, more important, didn't want one.

"In the end, Trump did to the NFL what he was able to do to the rest of America," says this official. "He was able to take advantage of our racial fault lines and weaknesses. Our owners were more than happy to be Donald Trump's NFL."

* * *

While most African American players in locker rooms intensely dislike Trump, the NFL ownership is different. The owner of the Patriots, Robert Kraft, gave Trump a Super Bowl ring in 2017 following the Patriots' Super Bowl LI win over the Atlanta Falcons.

When Trump began attacking the players publicly, he placed phone calls to some owners to get them to push players to stand, instead of kneel. One of those men was Jones. In fact, Trump called him four times.

"Please tell your players," Trump told Jones, according to a person familiar with the conversation, "to stand. They need to stand. Or your league will be in big trouble."

The difference between the players and owners was exemplified in a conversation between Goodell and union head DeMaurice Smith.

In one phone call, Goodell made it clear he wanted the players to stop protesting. But as ESPN first reported, Smith said no. "I don't have the power to tell our players what to do," he told Goodell. Nor did Smith have any inclination to. He didn't trust Goodell, and it's likely he never will. Players view Goodell as, essentially, an extension of ownership. To players, Goodell is one of *them*.

To illustrate how tense things had become, and how terrified some owners were that the protests might rip apart their league and end the profit-making machine that is professional football, there was a secret meeting between a small group of players and owners in late September 2017. To be clear, there were a small number of owners who genuinely cared about the players' concerns, and also made it clear they were not in support of the president.

There would be productive dialogue but, in many ways, that meeting—and the entire movement by the players—represented a truly American struggle. The players, in some ways, represent Americans who see Trump as a bigoted and divisive figure, with little understanding as to how anyone could support him, let alone vote for him. The owners represent Trump supporters: Americans who believe he looks out for the interest of the forgotten Americans.

As usual, as it has for so long, the NFL wasn't just about football. The sport represented America—for all its greatness and division.

* * *

We've already discussed numerous examples of this, but there's one other that exemplified the minefield so many had to navigate. In September 2017, prior to playing the Ravens on Sunday, two days after Trump's notorious remarks that any player who doesn't stand for the anthem should be cut from the team, mostly all of the Steelers players stayed in the locker room during the anthem to protest Trump's words. The only player who didn't was Alejandro Villanueva, a former Army Ranger who served in Afghanistan. He stood outside the locker room in the tunnel leading to the field.

That Monday, tensions in the Steelers locker room were still high. There was another team meeting about the anthem, at which point it was decided that the team would stand, on the field, during it. The entire episode shows how complicated this issue remains—even now.

* * *

One of the biggest signs that the NFL was terrified of Colin Kaepernick was the league's recruiting of rapper and music heavyweight Jay-Z.

For decades, much of Jay-Z's music, like large swaths of hip hop, was dedicated to pointing out various societal injustices involving people of color. One such injustice was police brutality. In 2016, after a number of police shootings, Jay-Z dropped the song "Spiritual," which addressed police brutality. "I made this song a while ago, I never got to finish it," Jay-Z wrote on the site Tidal. "I'm saddened and disappointed in THIS America—we should be further along. WE ARE NOT."

Later, however, there would be a different Jay-Z. Just several years after that song's release, the owner of the New England Patriots, Robert Kraft, convinced Jay-Z to meet with commissioner Roger Goodell. That meeting led to Jay-Z's Roc Nation, one of the most powerful entertainment companies in the world, pairing with the NFL and giving Jay-Z influence over the NFL's Super Bowl Halftime Show, which is watched by tens of millions of people every year.

Jay-Z's partnership with the NFL was viewed by Kaepernick, people close to him, and many others as a betrayal of those protesting. "Jay-Z claimed to be a supporter of Colin—wore his jersey, told people not to perform at the Super Bowl because of the treatment that the NFL did to Colin," said Eric Reid. "And now he's going to be a part owner . . . it's kind of despicable."

"I think we've moved past kneeling. I think it's time to go into actionable items," Jay-Z said. "So what are we going to do? Reach millions and millions of people, or we got stuck on Colin not having a job?"

"When has Jay-Z ever taken a knee, to come out and tell us we're past kneeling?" Reid said. "Yes, he's done a lot of great work, a lot of great social justice work, but for you to get paid to go into an NFL press conference and say that we're past kneeling? Again, asinine."

To some, Jay-Z was hired to give the NFL credibility among people of color (namely African Americans) that the league hadn't truly earned. "I feel like Jay-Z is giving them way too much of his cultural capital that they have not earned," Jemele Hill told the *New York Times*. "There has always been this tension of 'Will progress be made from working from the inside?' The things that Jay-Z is trying to accomplish, he doesn't need the NFL to do."

In an interview with the *New York Times* in January 2020, Jay-Z said, "We are two adult men who disagree on the tactic but are marching for the same cause."

The problem is that just isn't true, and the statement exemplifies how people—including, in this instance, Jay-Z—were either purposely confusing Kaepernick's message or failing to understand how the NFL didn't believe in the core of what he and others were saying.

There's a simple reason for the difference of beliefs. The NFL and Kaepernick didn't have the same mission, because Kaepernick's message was dramatically different from the NFL's. Once, while standing at his locker, Kaepernick said that "cops are getting paid leave for killing people. That's not right."

His main message was simple: I am drawing attention to the dire mistreatment of black people, particularly by law enforcement and the judicial system. Note that wording: *mistreatment of black people.*

The NFL, with its Inspire Change program, which funds glossy ads highlighting the experience of black people with law enforcement, had a different message. It's message? Let's chat about the issue.

Those are two drastically different things. Then, the NFL put Jay-Z as the face of its watered-down message.

"What nobody seems to explicitly want to say is, the issue that people had with Kaepernick was not that he didn't stand for the anthem," said ESPN's Bomani Jones on his show *The Right Time*. "It's that he explicitly said the reason that he did not was to protest the mistreatment of black people. That was the problem. That's why he's not in the league. That's why Inspire Change can exist as it does because Inspire Change is not saying black people are mistreated. Inspire Change is saying, 'We need to have a dialogue.' And I can't say explicitly that Jay-Z is not saying that black people are being mistreated, but this is the operation that he got his hands on. And I fear that when all this shakes out, Jay-Z is going to use the press to make himself look better, the NFL is going to use ads like this to make themselves look better, and the people they're claiming to help? Going to look exactly the same."

Jay-Z, in the same town hall with Goodell, said some of the contributing factors of unarmed people of color being shot was because of victims using excitable hand gestures and broken homes without fathers. Yes, he said that. Jay-Z actually said that.

Thus it appeared to many that the NFL was using a neat PR trick—and lots of money—to buy itself a racial hall pass with Jay-Z approval.

There were numerous moments like this one in the fight between the NFL and supporters of Kaepernick. His supporters (rightfully so) believe the NFL has never been held accountable for how it treated the former quarterback, and the belief of people like Jay-Z, who think it's time to move on from the quarterback's message. "He was done wrong," Jay-Z told the *New York Times*. "I would understand if it was three months ago. But it was three years ago and someone needs to say, 'What do we do now—because people are still dying?'"

There's also a larger issue at play, as I was told by several players who support Kaepernick. They believe that Jay-Z was also a conduit, and part of a flanking movement by the NFL to essentially co-opt Kaepernick's message, sanitize it, and repackage it as something more digestible to mainstream NFL fans.

The giveaway is the NFL's Inspire Change program. It's an initiative started by the league several years ago that allows current and former players to receive grants for whatever social justice cause they choose. A committee composed of players and team owners determines who gets the money and how much.

One thing you'll notice with the Inspire Change campaign is how there is no mention of Kaepernick. "Inspire Change is a shameless strategy for Commissioner Roger Goodell and the league's owners to pretend that they not only supported the movement to bring attention to police violence and systemic oppression all along," wrote Samer Kalaf in the *Washington Post*, "but that they were really the progenitors of the whole idea. Any player who accepts the deal on these rotten terms is welcome. The painfully obvious tell is that former San Francisco 49ers quarterback Colin Kaepernick is nowhere to be found."

In doing this, the NFL went back to an old playbook, as Kalaf wrote: "The NFL has a playbook for handling player activism. For years, the league was committed to promoting Breast Cancer Awareness Month in October, with pink splashed on seemingly every part of the football field, including coaches' gear, goal post padding and cheerleader pompoms. Former running back DeAngelo Williams, whose mother and four aunts died of the disease, asked the NFL if he could wear pink for the whole 2015 season, not just during October. His request was denied, because that would have been a violation of the uniform code. But the league had no problem making Williams the focus of a 30-second Football is Family ad highlighting how much it cares about stories like his.

"When the NFL was in a crisis in 2014 after a spate of players, most notably then–Baltimore Ravens running back Ray Rice, were charged with domestic violence and assault, it partnered with a group called No More to do something about its image problem. It gradually became evident that No More had no clearly defined purpose other than to sell merchandise with a special logo on it and facilitate an ad that had Eli Manning stare into a camera and try his best to look stern as he said, "No more." The follow-up ad, which aired during Super Bowl XLIX, featured 60 seconds of scenes from an empty but ominous household set to a tense 911 call. Sounds familiar."

Chapter 11

HEROES AND THE BOY KING

"There's that saying about sticking your neck out."

—Michael Bennett, to the author

During the two years that the anthem controversy reached its peak, from 2016 to 2018, Colin Kaepernick spent most of his days out of the spotlight; he refused to give opponents ammunition. The problem is, others were attempting to define him.

He continued to be called un-American in some parts of the right-wing media. His patriotism continued to be questioned. Social media still contained thousands of posts and memes criticizing and mocking him.

Not everyone felt this way about Kaepernick, yet many in the media did, which impacted how people viewed him. If members of the media were portraying him as a thug, despite the fact he was the total opposite, this meant a significant number of readers and viewers would believe the narrative.

It always seemed like Kaepernick was fighting—and many times, the fight had nothing to do with him. He didn't start these fights. Like many black men, we are born into the fight. Our existence in itself is a fight. A cop deems us a threat while sitting in our car. A clerk in a store deems us a thief. A sitting president deems us a threat.

So, who is Colin Kaepernick? He's a man called both a traitor—"Maybe he should find a country that works better for him," Trump said as a presidential candidate—and a hero—"He is the Muhammad Ali of this generation," the longtime civil rights activist Harry Edwards told *The New York Times*.

Ali once stated at a news conference, "I've said it once, and I will say it again. The real enemies of my people are right here. Not in Vietnam. I will not go 10,000 miles to continue the domination of white slave masters over the darker people of the Earth."

There's a belief (an accurate one) that no matter how Kaepernick handled his protest—kneeling, not kneeling, speaking, hand over heart, whatever—he would have received backlash. It's reminiscent of something Jackie Robinson wrote of baseball great Willie Mays in Robinson's book *Baseball Has Done It*: "I don't think anyone in or out of sports would accuse Willie Mays of offending white sensitivities. But when he was in California, whites refused to sell him a home in their community. They loved his talent, but didn't want him as a neighbor."

In other words, some people, like with Mays, only cared that Kaepernick could throw a football. Once he expressed himself beyond those parameters and demonstrated humanity, he became an enemy.

But he didn't care. At all. It was also more than that.

Kaepernick realized that his power as an NFL quarterback wasn't solely about making money. He could also monetize influence.

He could be the opposite of shut up and dribble.

* * *

Kaepernick is one of the most polarizing figures and was perhaps the second-most polarizing figure in the nation during the protest movement, second only to his most powerful critic, President Trump. Yet he lacked the bombast of Trump. In fact, Kaepernick is thoughtful, highly intelligent, and, until he began protesting, was actually somewhat shy.

Attempts to define Kaepernick have mostly failed, as few people actually know him. But for those of us who have met and spoken with him, as well as those close to him, he remains a simple person to digest. Kaepernick became aware of the racial injustices in this country at an early age—especially as a biracial son to white adoptive parents.

"We used to go on these summer driving vacations and stay at motels," Kaepernick told *US Weekly* in 2015. "And every year, in the lobby of every motel, the same thing always happened, and it only got worse as I got older and taller. It didn't matter how close I stood to my family, somebody would walk up to me, a real nervous manager, and say: 'Excuse me. Is there something I can help you with?'"

> This type of incident is, unfortunately, extremely common for biracial families with adoptive kids. In my case, I have darker skin, and my biracial adoptive daughter looks white. I've had people ask if I was her babysitter, nanny, and "guardian." Once, a police officer, during a traffic stop, and with my daughter in the back seat, asked me multiple times if I was her father. Then, the officer asked her. She was five-years-old at the time.

"I saw him transform, develop, whatever you want to call it," said John Bender, who played with Kaepernick at UNLV, to *The New York Times*. "Finding an identity was big for him, because in some aspects in life, he would get the racist treatment from white people because he was a black quarterback. And some people gave him the racist treatment because he was raised by a white family. So where does he fit in in all this?"

Kaepernick began taking courses from a University of California-Berkley professor named Ameer Hasan Loggins. The summer course was in black representation in popular culture. Kaepernick had long been smart and educated, but his "wokeness" was now in full bloom. One of the reasons why was a brilliant woman named Nessa Diab.

Speak to her for even a brief time, and her intelligence, humor, and strength emerges almost instantly. Diab is a syndicated radio host and MTV personality and has dated Kaepernick for over three years. She is an inspiration in her own right, especially due to her involvement in the Black Lives Matter movement. If Kaepernick was the king of the movement in the NFL, she was its queen.

It was Diab who introduced Kaepernick to Loggins. The two men would talk extensively about African American history and politics, with Loggins giving Kaepernick a list of books to read. It included *The Wretched of the Earth* by Frantz Fanon, *Black Feminist Thought: Knowledge, Consciousness, and the Politics of Empowerment* by Patricia Hill Collins, *Black Looks: Race and Representation* by bell hooks, and *The Mis-Education of the Negro* by Carter G. Woodson.

* * *

To many, the history of African Americans and other minorities fighting for civil rights in sports begins with Major League Baseball. This is understandable, since for so long, baseball was America's pastime, and Jackie Robinson breaking the color barrier is one the country's most important moments.

While baseball certainly has its ugly past, football fought hard to keep blacks marginalized. Decades after Jackie Robinson hung up his cleats, the NFL had essentially locked blacks out of many of its positions, and some of its teams. There was one team in particular that fought hard to keep blacks off its roster.

"We'll start signing Negroes," former Washington Redskins team owner George Preston Marshall, a staunch segregationist, once said, "when the Harlem Globetrotters start signing whites."

Football's fearless activists, now and in the past, were always met with intense resistance from ownership. Football players have been among the most docile in fighting owner authority, in part because of the sport's mentality that team comes before individual, but also because of the propagated notion that players are easily replaceable.

Players were always told to be grateful they were able to make millions playing a sport. Kaepernick became so enraged over the brutality he saw that he no longer cared about being grateful. Both Kaepernick and Trump used this emotion differently. Kaepernick, and other players who protested, no longer felt grateful to a nation that still discriminated against them. Trump did something else with that emotion when he attacked the players.

"I think Trump . . . wanted to play a certain kind of race card," said Gerald Early, the chair of the department of African and African American Studies at Washington University in St. Louis, to Slate.com, "because he was focusing on sports, where there are a high number of African Americans. And to his base, these African Americans who are very successful in these sports, are very highly paid, and so, it's easy for him to use them to many of the disaffected whites who are Trump supporters, to say, 'Look at these ungrateful black people.'

"I don't recall any incident where a sitting president went after a particular sports industry in the way that Trump did," Early added. "I mean, there have been politics in sports, of course. But the idea that an entire industry, an entire sport, would be attacked in this particular way is, to my mind, unprecedented."

* * *

After Tommie Smith and John Carlos raised gloved fists at the 1968 Olympics, the mainstream American media brutalized them. As author Howard Bryant notes in *The Heritage: Black Athletes, a Divided America, and the Politics of Patriotism*, *Newsweek* put Smith on its July 15, 1968, cover with the headline "The Angry Black Athlete."

"Two years earlier, when Jim Brown quit football," writes Bryant, "*Time* magazine ran a picture of him in fatigues, on the set of *The Dirty Dozen*, the World War II movie Brown was filming. Instead of comparing Brown to an American soldier, the magazine compared him to Che Guevara, the murdered Cuban revolutionary. Brent Musburger, who would go on to have a legendary broadcasting career despite harboring racist attitudes toward the very players he glamorized every weekend, would refer to Smith and Carlos as 'two dark-skinned storm troopers.'"

There was much more back then. Look at the reaction now from right-wing media to Kaepernick, and the similarities are hard to ignore.

* * *

We started with history and its importance. Some of that history of race and sports, just like in society, is bleak and ugly. But there are moments of decency and honor, and they occur all across the sports universe. One of them involved baseball greats John "Buck" O'Neil and Ty Cobb.

Cobb's foulness as a human being is well documented. We don't need to revisit it. What's remarkable is how some black players like O'Neil, who played in the same era as Cobb, never returned such vitriol. In fact, in a 2010 interview, O'Neil put people such ballplayers in wonderful perspective.

"Not only Ty Cobb, but any guy, in that era, white guy, was prejudiced," said O'Neil. "That was the way of life. He had been told all his life that he was superior to the black guy. Any black guy. Ty Cobb maybe had a fifth-grade education, but he felt he was superior to any black."

"But you don't condemn him for that?" he was asked. O'Neil sat forward in his seat.

> Who am I to condemn? They always ask me, "I know you hate people for what they did to you?" I say, "I never learned to hate." I hate cancer . . . I hate AIDS. I hate what the Klan would do. I hate what the skinheads would do. I hate what happened September the 11th. But I can't hate a human being. That's God's creature, and God never made anything ugly. You can get ugly if you wanna.' A lot of people did. But God didn't make you that way. Because somebody had to teach Ty Cobb how to be prejudiced. No baby [is] prejudiced. You teach these things. And actually, I feel sorry for the guy that hates me because I'm black. It doesn't hurt me. It hurts him. . . . Because

any way you put it, you're my brother. You're my sister. Just a different color.

Once the Trump era is long dead and history views Kaepernick for the hero he is, maybe we will see the country come back together. Maybe we will see togetherness and moments like this one involving baseball Hall of Famer Satchel Paige.

The story comes from the book *Veeck—As in Wreck: The Autobiography of Bill Veeck*. Veeck was a baseball showman and one of the greatest team builders in the sport's history. What he writes about Paige is something that hopefully can happen in the future, after Trump is gone, and Americans begin looking at each other as brothers and sisters again:

> His effect upon people is best shown, I think, in his relationship with Clint Courtney, the [St. Louis] Browns' hard-nosed catcher. Clint came from a poor farm district of Alabama, and the racial question was very strong with him.
>
> In the beginning, Courtney wouldn't even catch Satch in the bullpen. Then, I began to see him warming Satch up. Shortly afterwards, I could see them sitting side by side in the bullpen, talking. At last, Clint came up to the office and said, "I'd like to catch Paige."
>
> "Oh," I said. "Why the change?"
>
> "I like the guy," he said. "That Satch, he's quite a fellow. Just sitting out there talking to him, I've learned more about calling a game than I ever knew in my life."
>
> "Yeah," I said. "But what about this business that he's black?"
>
> "I guess that's right," he said. "But this is different."
>
> Later in the season, I dropped into an interracial joint I used to go to in Detroit—The Flame—and there, sitting at a table together, were Paige and Courtney.

"You know," Courtney said as I sat down, "it's a funny thing. My daddy is coming up when we get back to St. Louis. He's going to see me sitting in the bullpen talking to this Paige and he's gonna jump right over the fence and try to give me a whupping. But Satch and I have it figured out that the two of us can whup him no matter what happens."

This is the way Satch, just by being Satch, can affect a guy who didn't even want to warm him up.

Chapter 12

PURE VENGEANCE

"Mr. Trump, as long as I or my heirs are involved in the NFL, you will never be a franchise owner in the league."

—NFL Commissioner Pete Rozelle to Trump,
according to Jeff Pearlman's book *Football for a Buck*

One of the ironies of many NFL owners now supporting Donald Trump is that there was a time, not so long ago, when most of them thought he was total joke.

In fact, they despised him. They believed he was a liar, untrustworthy, and selfish (sounds familiar). In the end, the NFL rejected Trump—and not just rejected him, they laughed at him on his way out the door.

That rejection is an extremely important part of this story. It would factor into Trump taking such an aggressive and hostile stance toward the NFL and its players.

When Trump became owner of the New Jersey Generals of the United States Football League (USFL) in 1984, he intended to use that ownership as a launching pad into purchasing an NFL team.

151

That never happened. Instead, he was the biggest reason for why the USFL failed. The owners in that league despised him too.

"Trump wasn't merely disliked by his fellow owners; he was loathed and abhorred and detested," wrote Pearlman in 2018 in a blog about his book *Football for a Buck*, referring to the USFL owners. "The general take: Here was a selfish bully who desperately craved an NFL franchise, and viewed the USFL as a temporary (and disposable) vehicle toward that end. Trump memorably led the USFL's suicide march away from a spring season and toward the fall, and (much like now) his big words and loud voice and thuggish tendencies caused many lemming peers to follow."

The reason this is all important now is because it highlights one of Trump's defining characteristics: his world-class grudge-holding. That systemic keeping of lists of enemies was a key reason why Trump jumped into the protest fray.

Before a campaign event in 2015, he told reporters at a news conference, "When people treat me unfairly, I don't let them forget it."

His list of grudges, almost unending, even extend to dead heroes. When Senator John McCain, who consistently expressed that a Trump presidency was bad for America, died in 2018, Trump still demonstrated that his grudge against McCain was intact. "How long can President Donald Trump hold a grudge? A long time," wrote the *Salt Lake Tribune*. "While world leaders and politicos of every stripe issued statements honoring Sen. John McCain—longtime senator, Vietnam vet and POW, and maverick—Trump rejected a proposed statement praising the former GOP nominee who was often critical of the president. Instead, Trump tweeted a terse message that his thoughts and prayers were with the family."

It may seem odd, but Trump's grudge-holding and his attacking of Kaepernick intersect perfectly, like two interlocking puzzle pieces.

Trump mainly saw the NFL player protests as an opportunity to exploit America's racial divisions for political gain. He was almost destined to dislike Kaepernick.

There's another reason, however, why Trump attacked the NFL during the protests: it was payback for when the NFL rejected his attempt to purchase a team. As is his character, it was just another example of good old-fashioned score settling.

He saw it as an opportunity to injure the league that had so sternly told him to fuck off.

* * *

"Why did Trump get involved?" Kenny Stills said, after I asked him why he thought the president became so heavily invested in repudiating their movement. "I can't imagine any other president getting involved except to reach out to us and understand why we were doing what we were doing. Obama understood us. With Trump, he wanted to destroy the players. It seemed extremely personal."

That's because it was.

When Trump bought the Generals in 1984, his immediate goal became clear: he wanted to shift the USFL from a spring league to a fall one and directly take on the NFL. Other USFL owners wanted no part of that because, well, they weren't morons. Taking on the NFL on its own turf was like initiating a self-destruct sequence.

Trump's football instincts were actually pretty terrible, and his track record of making good decisions in that area is abysmal.

Trump had an opportunity to purchase the Dallas Cowboys for $50 million, but declined because he didn't think it was a good investment. "I could've bought an NFL team if I wanted to," Trump is quoted as saying in 1983, "but I'd rather create something from scratch. I feel sorry for the poor guy who is going to buy the Dallas Cowboys. It's a no-win situation for him, because if he wins, well, so what, they've won through the years, and if he loses . . . he'll be known to the world as a loser."

The Cowboys, purchased several years later by Jerry Jones, are now the world's most valuable sports franchise, according to *Forbes* magazine, worth approximately $5 billion.

Trump also apparently attempted to purchase the then Baltimore Colts in 1981. Though the bulk of this claim comes from the late Robert Irsay, who was, shall we say, not always familiar with the truth, he told the *Baltimore Sun* that a six-man group featuring former Washington coach George Allen, and led by Trump, made an offer for the Colts in 1981. Irsay said he rejected it.

When Trump finally got his football team, he ran it, and the entire USFL, into oblivion.

"We had a great league and a great idea," said Houston Gamblers owner Jerry Argovitz. "But then everyone let Donald Trump take over. It was our death."

Trump was so obsessed with impressing, and beating, the NFL that facts didn't matter. Trump didn't push for the fall move because it was good for the USFL. Trump pushed it because he wanted the NFL to notice the Generals. Or, perhaps, only him. Then, they'd welcome the Generals into the NFL. Or, perhaps, only him.

Eventually, Trump convinced the USFL's owners to file an anti-trust lawsuit against the NFL. A jury ruled against the NFL but awarded the USFL just $1 in damages. Since it was an anti-trust case, that amount was tripled to a whopping $3.

It's possible, even probable, that moment cemented a grudge from a man who holds them for years. Or, maybe, holds them forever.

* * *

From September 2017 to September 2018, Trump tweeted about the NFL 26 times, criticizing the league over everything from the protests to the NFL's ratings. The Grudge Effect was in full swing.

"Wow, NFL first game ratings are way down over an already really bad last year comparison," he tweeted on September 9, 2018. "Viewership declined 13%, the lowest in over a decade. If the players stood proudly for our Flag and Anthem, and it is all shown on broadcast, maybe ratings could come back? Otherwise worse!"

Trump's bitterness toward the NFL would only intensify in 2014, when he attempted to purchase the Buffalo Bills but was beaten out by the team's current owners, the Pegula family, who paid $1.4 billion to acquire the franchise.

At the time, as Trump was attempting to purchase the Bills, one owner, who asked to remain anonymous, told me the support for Trump from owners "was between 0 and 0.0001. He wasn't viewed as a serious candidate."

After his bid failed, Trump took to Twitter: "Wow," he wrote, "@NFL ratings are down big league. Glad I didn't get the Bills. Rather be lucky than good."

The attacks on the league from Trump would continue for years and still do to this day.

"The NFL should have its non-profit status immediately revoked while at the same time ending the giant tax scam which makes teams so valuable," he tweeted in September 2014.

"The @nfl games are so boring now that actually, I'm glad I didn't get the Bills," he tweeted in October 2014. "Boring games, too many flags, too soft!"

The attacking of the NFL now wasn't new or even a restart. It was part of a continuation of getting even. The NFL was like McCain, or Mitt Romney, or Obama, or dozens of other people or institutions Trump saw as the enemy. The only difference was now he was the most powerful person in the world, and even the mighty NFL was an easy target.

What I've heard repeatedly from team and league officials now is how much Trump terrifies them. It's not just the tweets. It's how they fear he'll use his power to not only attack the sport on a social media level but also hurt them in more substantial ways. They don't know how he'd do that. They are just fearful he will.

And they're right to be scared.

* * *

None of this is to say that every player or person in the NFL agreed with Kaepernick or the player protests. Or even that every player or person in the NFL felt an increased sense of hostility during the Trump era. In fact, some in the NFL love Trump. One of his biggest backers is former Buffalo Bills and New York Jets coach, and current ESPN analyst, Rex Ryan.

Ryan was the head coach of the Bills in 2016, and speaking on behalf of Trump at a rally on April 16 of that year, with Trump standing nearby, Ryan, who would later became an ESPN analyst, sang his praises:

> There's so many things I admire about Mr. Trump, but one thing I really admire about him is—you know what—he'll say what's on his mind. And so many times, you'll see people—a lot of people—want to say the same thing. But there's a big difference: They don't have the courage to say it. They all think it, but they don't have the courage to say it. And Donald Trump certainly has the courage to say it.

Not everyone in the Bills organization liked Trump, or that Ryan backed him in such a high-profile manner. One Bills defensive player, who asked not to be identified for fear of repercussions from the NFL, said when he learned Ryan had spoken at Trump's rally, he simply couldn't believe it. "Rex is such an open-minded guy, a really good person," said the player. "But the fact he could back someone as closed-minded as Trump genuinely shocked me."

The player, who is black, told me at the time of the speech that "some of the African American players on the team weren't happy about Rex doing that."

Three years later, after initially telling me that, the player says his feelings remain the same.

Later, it would be discovered just how divisive Trump was in the Buffalo locker room. There were dozens of arguments over Trump in 2016—at times getting heated. Players estimated there were about a half-dozen Trump supporters, including Richie Incognito, the notorious bully who was kicked off the Dolphins and was once accused of sexual assault. Incognito was a proud and vocal Trump supporter, and defended the president whenever any of his teammates spoke disparagingly about him.

"I think that he can help this nation get back to a world superpower," Incognito told Tyler Dunne of *Bleacher Report* in 2016. "Where I think he could help is putting us first again and having that—it's my mentality, too—having that tough attitude where you put America first and everyone's thinking we're the greatest nation in the world. *Don't mess with America.* That toughness is where I identify with him."

I polled 43 players across the NFL before the election, and the results mirrored much of America. Twenty of twenty-two black players said they planned to vote for Hillary Clinton, two black players said they planned to vote for Trump, and twenty-one of twenty-one white players said they planned to vote for Trump.

Two years after the election, in 2018, I polled thirty-five players from across the league (including two Bills players)—nineteen black and sixteen white—and asked if they approved or disapproved of Trump. The results were similar to the original poll, and again broke down along racial lines. Like the original poll, these results were far from scientific, but telling nonetheless. From those I spoke with, eighteen of nineteen African American players said they viewed Trump unfavorably. All of the white players said they viewed Trump favorably.

One white respondent said he backed Trump because he believed "America was in decline and Trump was fixing the country." One black player said that, "I dislike Trump because I feel like his rhetoric puts my life in danger, and my son's life."

What's not known generally about NFL teams is that they often lean conservative. At least 40 to 50 percent of the league, by some players' estimates, believes Republicans do more to eradicate higher taxes, thus protecting more of their earnings. Trump has had supporters in NFL locker rooms for the same reasons he does outside them: many players said they appreciated his blunt talk and supported his promises to decimate terrorists, build walls, and strengthen the economy.

Trump, of course, wasn't just a topic in the Bills' locker room. He forced more discussion, and division, across all locker rooms (like he did across America) because even white supporters who backed him hated some of the things he said.

In Oakland, players gathered in small groups to discuss Trump's latest racist remark or controversial press conference. In Chicago, some white players defended him as a breath of fresh air, only to receive stern pushback from their black teammates. In Tennessee, the Titans players would argue about Trump, sometimes intensely. "We had some very heated debates in that locker room about Trump," said former Titans defensive back and current Brown Jason McCourty. "They would get intense. I always walked away, though, feeling encouraged because we could disagree about that so strongly but still be teammates."

Black players who might otherwise back a more conservative candidate said they have abandoned Trump because they view him as anti-black. Multiple players cited Trump's embrace of birtherism—the lie that President Obama isn't a natural-born citizen—as one of several reasons they dislike him.

"A lot of black players believe saying the first black president isn't really American is racist as fuck," one player explained.

Recalled another player: "I was talking Trump and Hillary with a white teammate, and the conversation was fine. Things got a little heated when he said, 'Trump isn't racist.' I don't know how anyone doesn't see how that's just not true. We talked about that statement for two days.

"We were taking a break during practice maybe four days or so after our last conversation about Trump," the player continued. "He came up to me and said, 'Here's why Trump's not racist and Hillary is.' Then we argued for another day. It was sort of heated again."

One of the things that Trump did, both as a candidate and as president, was cause black players to open up old wounds. Trump's words and actions forced them to relive ugly memories from their past, and in an odd way, reliving those moments caused some of the players to unify against the president.

The fights between the players and Trump was rooted in the president himself. He divided locker rooms and families as a candidate, not just as president. Players viewed him as using them to fire up his extremist base. If you're looking for why players rallied to oppose Trump when they never rallied before to oppose any political figure in anywhere close to these numbers, look no further than that reason. They didn't feel that Trump was solely being racist. They felt he was being repugnantly and manipulatively so. Many black players, like many black Americans, had experienced bigotry. But to them, Trump was different.

* * *

Let's take one last trip back to the election run-up, and back to the NFL locker rooms. In a league that is predominantly black but where anything-goes banter is encouraged and racial lines can be blurred, perhaps the most striking find in interviews with players is, in certain cases, what was left unsaid. "Black guys will talk about it to each other," ESPN analyst and two-time Super Bowl champion Damien Woody said to me about Trump in 2016. "White guys may talk about it to each other. But I think white players . . . tap around it with black players.

"The locker room normally isn't politically correct," Woody said. "I know from talking to players things are different when it comes to Trump."

Woody explained that white players were hesitant to talk about Trump because "a white player may parrot something Trump says, and the black player may think, 'Oh, that's how you feel?' And it could cause problems."

Those problems unfolded across the NFL. As Trump became the presumptive nominee, two NFC teammates—a right-leaning offensive lineman and a left-leaning linebacker—began to re-examine their friendship.

They had been teammates or four years. Their wives talked on occasion. Their kids sometimes played together. They sat next to each other in team meetings and went to dinner several times a month. They often joked that politics were off-limits because of their disparate viewpoints. Then, after their first offseason team workout that spring before the election, the lineman revealed he would be voting for Trump—and everything changed.

The linebacker, a supporter of presidential candidate Hillary Clinton, began finding excuses for not going to dinner. The families stopped talking. When the lineman confronted his now former friend, he recalls receiving a blunt response: "I can't be friends with anyone who would vote for Donald Trump. I'm sorry."

Some of the dynamics changed after Trump was elected, and this is where the future begins. Conversations started across the NFL months into the Trump presidency because they had to. Trump, and what he means to the country, could only stay under the surface for so long.

Epilogue

BEAUTIFULLY HISTORICAL

The team executive that, in 2016, told me how so much of the NFL despised Kaepernick because of his protest and how he'd never play professional football again, was back on the phone. He had more to say.

It was a day before Kaepernick was scheduled to work out for NFL teams in Atlanta, on November 16, 2019. He had considered sending a scout to watch the quarterback, but then decided not to. Why, you may ask? "It would have been a total waste of time," he said.

It has been remarkable how accurate this executive has been in predicting what would happen to Kaepernick. Besides accurately predicting his blacklisting, he also saw just how vicious the venom toward the quarterback would be from ownership and large swaths of the league. He also understood how much fear Kaepernick would generate within the NFL, as there had never been a player (the executive said years ago) who wasn't scared of losing his job. "This made Colin a whole different animal to owners, who use money and NFL jobs as threats. He couldn't be bought, so the only thing the NFL could do was demonize and then banish him. Make him an example to others in the league now, and to future players."

So when Kaepernick and the NFL arranged for him to work out for NFL teams in November 2019, this executive, at the time, predicted the workout would never happen. He was right again.

The entire thing was a sham. It began with a disagreement between the NFL and Kaepernick's camp about even where to hold the event. It was originally supposed to be in Atlanta, on the home field of the Falcons. About one hour before he was supposed to begin throwing, his camp moved the workout to a local area high school field. The heart of the disagreement was about a lack of trust, and it was understandable why Kaepernick had none in the NFL.

The league didn't want media to attend the workout; Kaepernick did because he wanted full transparency. Kaepernick's attorneys also had issue with some of the contractual language the NFL wanted to use for the workout. There were other issues, but the core was, again, about trust. There was none.

In the end, seven teams attended: the Lions, Eagles, Chiefs, Jets, Redskins, 49ers, and Titans. Once the workout started, it was obvious that little had changed with him. The power in his arm was still there, his touch was good, and he was in excellent physical condition. ESPN's Adam Schefter reported that a team executive told him Kaepernick's arm talent was "elite." One person in attendance told me that, based on the workout and his past history, Kaepernick was in the top 15 to 20 best quarterbacks in football. When asked, then, why didn't his team sign Kaepernick, he said, "My owner would never let me do it." Why did he attend if there was little, or no chance, he'd be allowed to sign Kaepernick? "There's a chance, a really small one, my owner would let me do it if all of our quarterbacks were injured."

After the workout, Kaepernick spoke to the media but didn't take questions:

> Let me start by saying, I appreciate y'all coming out. That means a lot to me. Our biggest thing with everything today is making sure we had transparency with what went on. We weren't getting that elsewhere, so we came out here.
>
> It's important that y'all are here. Y'all been attacked for the last three years, you continue to be attacked. We appreciate what y'all do, we appreciate you being here today, we appreciate the work you do for the people in telling the truth. That's what we want in everything.
>
> I've been ready for three years. I've been denied for three years. We all know why I came out here today and showed it in front of everybody. We have nothing to hide.
>
> So we're waiting for the 32 owners, the 32 teams, Roger Goodell, all of them to stop running, stop running from the truth, stop running from the people. Around here, we're ready to play, we're ready to go anywhere, my agent Jeff Nalley is ready to talk to any team. I'll interview with any team at any time.
>
> I've been ready. I'm staying ready. And I'll continue to be ready. To all the people that came out today to support, I appreciate y'all, I love y'all. To the people that aren't here, I'm thinking of you, I appreciate you supporting from where you are. We'll continue to give you updates as we hear. We'll be waiting to hear from Roger Goodell, the NFL, 32 teams. We'll let you know if we hear from them.
>
> The ball's in their court. We're ready to go.

* * *

After that workout, in February 2020, for the first time in several years, Kaep gave an extensive interview, and even just the news of who he gave that interview to said a lot about him.

Kaepernick spoke with longtime NFL writer Jarrett Bell, who has covered the NFL for *USA Today* for decades. Bell is one of the smartest and most talented people in the sports journalism business. Kaepernick of course recognized that, but picking Bell had another purpose. Kaepernick wanted an African American writer, which Bell is. For many of us who cover the NFL, it's rare for a black player to purposefully seek out a black journalist for an exclusive interview. Most of the time, black players seek out white reporters. It's just a fact (and the reasons for this are too numerous to cite here and would fill another book). Kaepernick decided otherwise, and the move was another way that he saw the world: compassionately, realistically, but also unabashedly pro-black.

What Kaepernick told Bell was fairly remarkable. He was finishing his book, due for publication in the fall of 2020, and had started his own publishing company, Kaepernick Publishing, which paired with Audible and was dedicated to showcasing the talents of people of color. Kaepernick had long backed up his talk with action, and here he was doing it again.

* * *

One remnant from the protests is that Kaepernick still doesn't have a job in the NFL. "Colin is a pioneer," said Andrew Brandt, a former NFL front office executive, to the *Guardian*. "He is a beacon for other athletes. We can all talk about his impact. But he's also not getting to do what he wants, which is play football. He has been ostracized."

"You've had people who have gotten DUIs coming back to the league," said Lou Moore, a history professor at Grand Valley State University and author of *We Will Win the Day: The Civil Rights Movement, the Black Athlete, and the Quest for Equality*, again to the *Guardian*. "Michael Vick came back to the league after dog fighting."

"The way the NFL works is, if you are good and can help a team, we will bring you in. Kaepernick is clearly good enough. And he didn't come back. That says a lot about what the teams think about him. And the fact that he had to know that [protesting] could cost him his career—and he still did it—says a lot about him."

Kaepernick's beliefs were powerful and sincere but, mostly, they were unapologetic. He didn't seek permission from whites to have them, and he ignored some of the people the media used as counterweights, names like Ray Lewis and Mike Vick. Most of all, more than anything, Kaepernick is honorable, and honorable men and women many times cannot be rerouted or deterred. They are indefatigable.

One of many ironies about Kaepernick is that, outside of NFL owners' boxes and certain fan segments, he was viewed as a hero. In 2018 he was awarded the W. E. B. Du Bois Medal, Harvard's highest honor in African and African American studies. Among the other honorees that year were comedian Dave Chappelle, artist Kehinde Wiley (who painted the official portrait of former president Barack Obama), and Equal Justice Initiative founder and executive director Bryan Stevenson. Past winners include Muhammad Ali, Maya Angelou, Oprah Winfrey, and civil rights leader and congressman John Lewis. That same year, Amnesty International named Colin Kaepernick its 2018 Ambassador of Conscience, the human rights group's highest honor. "How can you stand for the national anthem of a nation that preaches and propagates 'freedom and justice for all' that is so unjust to so many of the people living there?" Kaepernick said at the award ceremony in Amsterdam. "Racialized oppression and dehumanization is woven into the very fabric of our nation—the effects of which can be seen in the lawful lynching of black and brown people by the police, and the mass incarceration of black and brown lives in the prison industrial complex."

These awards came several years after his 49ers teammates awarded him the Len Eshmont Award. Established in 1957 after the death of Eshmont, the award is voted on by the San Francisco players. The award was given after the 2016 season, when Kaepernick started kneeling, and was won previously by some of the biggest names in NFL (and 49ers) history, including Joe Montana, Jerry Rice, and Steve Young.

Take all of the previously mentioned factors—racial tensions, an errant perception that the protesters were anti-police or anti-military—and combine them with a huckster president willing to exploit them, and you see why Kaepernick's protest, despite its benign nature, generated such ire.

The protest movement's impact, however, goes beyond Kaepernick and is everlasting. The movement didn't just bring awareness to the plague that is police brutality or a justice system that is weighted against people of color and the economically disadvantaged. The movement likely saved lives. It's possible the kneeling caused a police officer who might have otherwise acted with brutality, or worse, to maybe rethink his or her actions. Maybe it caused that officer to experience something as simple as a second thought.

That will always be the legacy of Colin Kaepernick, Eric Reid, Kenny Stills, and the numerous others who took a knee. It is a legacy of bravery, sacrifice, and honor. There will always be people who will say otherwise, but only the dishonest would say differently.

What these men did was also about the future and a realization that the fight isn't over. "What we're trying to get done is not going to happen overnight, and it's definitely not going to change with us—there will have to be another wave of players to carry the torch," receiver Michael Thomas said to *Bleacher Report* in 2018. Thomas also spoke of a conversation he'd one day have with his young daughter about his activism.

"I'll be real with her—just like, 'Your father was fighting for change. He wanted a better America and a better society for you and all the kids that were coming up after you,'" he said. "Knowing my daughter, just who she is now and the way she's been brought up, I know she'll be proud of me."

Some of the players protested while enduring unfathomable tragedy. As *Bleacher Report* noted, 49ers wide receiver Marquis Goodwin joined the movement in 2016 despite losing his son, born prematurely, and his father passing away just a few weeks after that. "I tried to avoid kneeling, just because a lot of people who didn't understand felt like it was disrespecting the country," Goodwin told *BR*. "But that wasn't the case."

"What we [Goodwin and his wife] went through gave me a different view on how I should feel. Eventually, I always knew I would take a knee, but when my wife was pregnant I had to start making decisions not only for me, but for her and our future kid. Obviously, we lost our kid, but moving forward I have to fight for my legacy and my future family. I gotta do what's right."

There's also a disturbing and frightening part of this story. It's that the NFL wanted to teach players a lesson: take too bold a step and you will pay a price. And you know what? The NFL got away with doing just that. Kaepernick is out of football, and it would be a stunner if a team ever signed him.

We started this story with Stills and something he said is something we should end with. He told the *Guardian* in 2019:

> Colin Kaepernick has played a really big part in helping open my eyes. He's influenced me and everything I've done from the time I first took a knee on September 11, 2016, to now. [Kaepernick] showed me that as athletes, there is something we can do. We can use our platform to inform other people what needs to change. To help people who don't have a voice be heard.
>
> People definitely ask me to stick to sports, and I totally understand where they are coming from. You want to be entertained, and get away from all the things that are happening. But that is also coming from a place of privilege.
>
> How do you think people feel who have lost kids to police brutality? Don't you think they want to live their lives and be entertained like something never happened to them? I still catch passes and touchdowns and the games still go on—but these things are happening to human beings. It shouldn't be hard to have a little bit of empathy.

BLACK LIVES MATTER
June 2020

Four years ago, when I started this book, I never imagined something that happened on June 5, 2020, would ever occur. On that remarkable day, the NFL apologized to the players who had spent the previous four years protesting. The league apologized to football's fearless activists. No one saw this coming. Furthermore, commissioner Roger Goodell released a video-taped statement:

> It has been a difficult time for our country, in particular, black people in our country. First, my condolences to the families of George Floyd, Breonna Taylor, Ahmaud Arbery, and all the families who have endured police brutality. We, the National Football League, condemn racism and the systematic oppression of black people. We, the National Football League, admit we were wrong for not listening to NFL players earlier, and encourage all to speak out and peacefully protest. We, the National Football League, believe black lives matter.
>
> I personally protest with you and want to be part of the much-needed change in this country. Without black players, there would be no National Football League, and the protests around the country are emblematic of the centuries of silence, inequality, and oppression of black players, coaches, fans, and

staff. We are listening. I am listening. And I will be reaching out to players who have raised their voices and others on how we can improve and go forward for a better and more united NFL family.

Roger Goodell, the man who, along with most of NFL ownership and a swath of team executives, essentially thwarted the protest movement, diminished it, tried to cut it off at the knees, was now embracing it. Goodell, who had figuratively given the middle finger to Kaepernick, was now saying Black Lives Matter.

This wasn't just an extraordinary moment—this was the twilight zone. In the span of one week—unfortunately due to the horrific murder of George Floyd—the conversation around football's fearless activists had shifted.

There was just one thing missing from Goodell's apology. It was one person's name: Colin Kaepernick.

Not mentioning the leader of the protest movement, the man who lost everything initiating it, is like talking about the moon landing without mentioning Neil Armstrong.

Nonetheless, the NFL, because it was forced to, traveled light years with Goodell's apology, and to understand just how far the league went, let's go back to the beginning.

* * *

A series of high-profile shootings of unarmed African American men, particularly the killing of Michael Brown in Ferguson, Missouri, on August 9, 2014, began to become a persistent—and ugly—part of American life. As a result, the Black Lives Matter movement, which was founded about a year earlier, gained momentum. The killings, and the movement, caught the attention of Kaepernick. He began protesting in 2016.

Trump, as a presidential candidate, railed against Kaepernick and the NFL protesters, and then used the power of the presidency to assail them while bullying the NFL into squashing the movement. Cowboys owner Jerry Jones, the most powerful owner in the league, threatened to bench any player who didn't stand for the anthem. After that threat became public, Trump, on October 9, 2017, tweeted: "A big salute to Jerry Jones, owner of the Dallas Cowboys, who will BENCH players who disrespect our Flag. Stand for the Anthem or sit for game!"

Most players relented, and stood, fearing they would be blackballed. "At that time when Kaepernick was taking a knee, I had the same thought that 85.9 percent of the league thought at that moment: 'If I get down on one knee in front of this stadium, I am fired,'" Bears defensive lineman Akiem Hicks told the *Chicago Tribune* in June 2020. "My job, my career, my life is over. I will be blackballed. And then to come out on the other end and watch it actually happen to Kaepernick, it just tells me my feelings were real."

Trump's hateful words and disdain of the protests, the NFL embracing Trump's rhetoric, and the blackballing of Kaepernick eventually destroyed the protest movement.

However, as Kaepernick had warned, the murders of unarmed black men by law enforcement continued. The most transformative of them all happened on May 25, 2020, when a white Minneapolis police officer kneeled on the neck of a handcuffed George Floyd for almost nine minutes, killing him.

Floyd's death culminated in protests across the nation and world, composing of millions of people. This forced the NFL to change its position.

In June 2020, three vital things occurred that, in some ways, changed the course of NFL history. First, NFL players, once scared to protest, began expressing their anger on social media, and many joined protesters on the streets. The fear some players had during the protest movement was replaced by anger and disgust.

A symbol of the players' newfound bravery, and fury, happened when some of the league's most notable players took part in a video that was as emotional as it was groundbreaking. The video begins with Saints wide receiver Michael Thomas speaking into the camera.

"It's been 10 days since George Floyd was brutally murdered," he said.

"How many times do we need to ask you to listen to your players?" asked Chiefs safety Tyrann Mathieu.

"What will it take?" asked Cardinals receiver DeAndre Hopkins.

"For one of us to be murdered by police brutality?" asked Browns receiver Jarvis Landry.

"What if I was George Floyd?" asked Cardinals cornerback Patrick Peterson.

"If I was George Floyd," said Giants running back Saquon Barkley.

"What if I was George Floyd?" asked Browns receiver Odell Beckham Jr.

Then, the players, including huge names like Kansas City quarterback Patrick Mahomes and Dallas running back Ezekiel Elliott, make these statements individually: "I am George Floyd . . . I am Breonna Taylor . . . I am Ahmaud Arbery . . . I am Eric Garner . . . I am Laquan McDonald . . . I am Tamir Rice . . . I am Trayvon Martin . . . I am Walter Scott . . . I am Michael Brown Jr . . . I am Samuel DuBose . . . I am Frank Smart . . . I am Phillip White . . . I am Jordan Baker."

The players ended the video with an unmistakable message to the NFL. Part of it stated, "We will not be silenced. We assert our right to peacefully protest."

Second, Saints quarterback Drew Brees, one of the most popular players in football, did an interview with Daniel Roberts of Yahoo! Finance on June 3 in which he dismissed player protests. "Well, I will never agree with anybody disrespecting the flag of the United States of America or our country," he said.

"Let me just tell you what I see or what I feel when the National Anthem is played and when I look at the flag of the United States. I envision my two grandfathers who fought for this country during World War II, one in the Army, and one of the Marine Corps, both risking their lives to protect our country and to try to make our country and this world a better place."

Brees had fallen into the same chasm that opponents of the protests did. Protesters had stated repeatedly that they were not protesting the flag, police, or the military. Brees also displayed a startling lack of historical knowledge. Black people fought in the second World War. But, unlike Brees's grandfathers, they returned to an America that shunned them, beat them, murdered them, and excluded them from the GI Bill, which transferred massive amounts of wealth to white veterans.

Brees's words infuriated fellow players—including Saints team-mates—forcing Brees to apologize multiple times.

Third, Trump, never failing to exploit divisions (particularly racial ones), chastised Brees for apologizing. Trump also revived the oldie but goodie that everyone should stand for the flag.

"I am a big fan of Drew Brees," Trump tweeted on June 5. "I think he's truly one of the best quarterbacks, but he should not have taken back his original stance on honoring our magnificent Flag. OLD GLORY is to be revered, cherished and flown high . . . We should be standing up straight and tall, ideally with a salute, or a hand on heart. There are other things you can protest, but not our Great American Flag—NO KNEELING!"

Six hours after Trump's tweet to Brees, the quarterback responded:

> Through my ongoing conversations with friends, teammates, and leaders in the black community, I realize this is not an issue about the American flag. It has never been. We can no longer use the flag to turn people away or distract them from the real issues that face our black communities.
>
> We did this back in 2017, and regretfully I brought it back with my comments this week. We must stop talking about the flag and shift our attention to the real issues of systemic racial injustice, economic oppression, police brutality, and judicial & prison reform. We are at a critical juncture in our nation's history! If not now, then when?
>
> We as a white community need to listen and learn from the pain and suffering of our black communities. We must acknowledge the problems, identify the solutions, and then put this into action. The black community cannot do it alone. This will require all of us.

Trump had forced Brees to pick a side—and it was *not* the side Trump thought it would be.

In fact, Brees's sudden transformation seemed more than trans-actional—it felt genuine. Several days later Drew's wife, Brittany, posted a remarkable statement on Instagram that seemed anything but fake. It's run here in its entirety, as it is one of the most impactful things any white person stated during the entire four years of the protest movement.

Her post started with two quotes from Martin Luther King: "In the end we will remember not the words of our enemies but the silence of our friends," and "Not only will we have to repent for the sins of bad people, but we also will have to repent for the appalling silence of good people."

Her own words began: "WE ARE THE PROBLEM."

> I write this with tears in my eyes and I hope you all hear our hearts. I have read these quotes and scripture 1000 times and every time I read it and the words sink into my heart. I think yes this is what it's all about. Only until the last few days, until we experienced the death threats we experienced the hate did I realize that these words were speaking directly to us. How could anyone who knows us or has had interactions with us think that Drew or I have a racist bone in our body? But that's the whole point. Somehow we as white America, we can feel good about not being racist, feel good about loving one an another [*sic*] as God loves us. We can feel good about educating our children about the horrors of slavery and history. We can read books to our children about Martin Luther King, Malcolm X., Hank Aaron, Barack Obama, Rosa parks, Harriet Tubman and feel like we are doing our part to raise our children to love, be unbiased and with no prejudice. To teach them about all of the African Americans that have fought for and risked their lives against racial injustice.

Somehow as white Americans we feel like that checks the box of doing the right thing. Not until this week did Drew and I realize THAT THIS IS THE PROBLEM. To say "I don't agree with disrespecting the flag" I now understand was also saying I don't understand what the problem really is, I don't understand what you're fighting for, and I'm not willing to hear you because of our preconceived notions of what that flag means to us.

That's the problem we are not listening, white America is not hearing. We're not actively LOOKING for racial prejudice. We have heard stories from men and women we have known and loved for years about the racism that occurred in their lives stories that were never shared or talked about because somehow they were considered normal. To all of our friends and anyone we hurt, we will do better. We want to do better, we want to HEAR you, and we will fight for you because thinking we are not part of the problem is checking the box it means we are not doing enough. It's our job to educate ourselves. We are sorry.

Overall, the NFL's attitude toward protests and the Black Lives Matter movement had changed more in one week than it had in the previous four years. In a swift and decisive pincer movement, the league—like Brees—had opened its eyes. It was, officially and unbelievably—at least for the moment—now anti-Trump.

It took the brutal videotaped murder of a black man to do it, but it finally happened.

There are a handful of key moments in the history of the NFL: integration, the 1958 championship game between the Baltimore Colts and New York Giants, the AFL-NFL merger before the 1970 season, the Dolphins' perfect season; the league post–September 11, and a few others.

Kaepernick's protest, and the remarkable events in June 2020, will go down as some of the league's most vital historical events.

It was also one of the NFL's most important learning experiences. While a number of owners supported Trump, the most important factor for the league was fear. Fear of Trump. His tweets. His supporters. Even though the cause was righteous and just. Fear caused the NFL to shun its own players who were simply, peacefully, drawing attention to the fact that Black Lives Matter.

Fear put the NFL on the wrong side of history.

And then there was Kaepernick, who exemplified fearlessness.

I want to go back to something he said to *USA Today* in 2016; it was always lost, often purposefully so, amid Kaepernick's message. "The media painted this as I'm anti-American, anti-men-and-women of the military and that's not the case at all," he said. "I realize that men and women of the military go out and sacrifice their lives and put themselves in harm's way for my freedom of speech and my freedoms in this country and my freedom to take a seat or take a knee so I have the utmost respect for them. Once again, I'm not anti-American. I love America."

It's a cliché, but it's accurate to say one person—or a small group of people—can make a monumental difference. For all of the NFL's billions, and power, and rich owners, and public relations machinery, it wasn't the league that led.

No, it was football's fearless activists.

CHARITIES OF INTERVIEWED PLAYERS

Below is a list of some of the players interviewed for this book and the charities they run. The latter is listed because the work they do is important and, in many cases, vastly underrecognized. Not every player interviewed is listed, but all have donated their time and money to help those in need.

Doug Baldwin

Doug Baldwin Family Combine: "Doug Baldwin, the City of Renton, Renton School District, and HealthPoint have created a partnership to build a state-of-the-art community center in the Cascade/Benson neighborhood. Their vision is to provide youth and families in the area with a community center that offers health, wellness, recreational and educational opportunities." www.db89combine.com

Michael Bennett

The Bennett Foundation: "Michael and Pele Bennett established The Bennett Foundation with their three daughters, Peyton, Blake, and Ollie, adopting programming to direct their efforts towards losing gaps and ensuring that children and families are empowered

to make social and behavioral changes to improve their health status and well-being. The Bennett Foundation educates underserved children and communities through free, accessible programming in Hawaii, Washington, and Texas."
www.thebennettfoundation.org

Malcolm Jenkins

The Malcolm Jenkins Foundation: "To effectuate positive change in the lives of youth, particularly those in underserved communities. The charity provides resources, innovative opportunities, and experiences that will help youth succeed in life and become contributing members of their communities. The Foundation aims to be a world-class organization that is positioned as a leader in having a positive and lasting impact in the lives of youth it serves in communities of New Jersey, Louisiana, Ohio and Pennsylvania."
www.themalcolmjenkinsfoundation.org

Colin Kaepernick

Like many of those listed, Colin Kaepernick has donated his money and time to numerous charities and foundations. Two of them are described here:

100 Suits for 100 Men: Founded in 2011 by Kevin Livingston, "The mission of 100 Suits for 100 Men is to help underprivileged men and women improve their role in society, build dignity and self-esteem, foster self-sufficiency, dispel stereotypes, and promote community involvement in order to build each other up."
www.100suits.org

Know Your Rights Camp: "Our mission is to advance the liberation and well-being of Black and Brown communities through education, self-empowerment, mass-mobilization and the creation of new systems that elevate the next generation of change leaders." www.knowyourrightscamp.com

Marshawn Lynch
Fam1st Family Foundation: "Fam1st Family Foundation is focused on the underserved youth, aiming to build new generations of innovative thinkers to create solutions for the future of Oakland & the World."
www.fam1stfamilyfoundation.org

Eric Reid
Know Your Rights Camp: "Our mission is to advance the liberation and well-being of Black and Brown communities through education, self-empowerment, mass-mobilization and the creation of new systems that elevate the next generation of change leaders." www.knowyourrightscamp.com

Aaron Rodgers
Aaron Rodgers supports numerous charities, including (but not limited to): *Red Cross* (www.redcross.org), *Make-A-Wish Foundation* (www.wish.org), *Jimmy Fund* (www.jimmyfund.org), *Boys & Girls Clubs of America* (www.bgca.org), *Feeding America* (www.feedingamerica.org), and *Shriners Hospitals for* Children (www.shrinershospitalsforchildren.org).

Richard Sherman

Blanket Coverage Foundation: "Blanket Coverage, the Richard Sherman Family Foundation, was formed in 2013 by Richard Sherman to provide students in low-income communities with school supplies and clothing so they can more adequately achieve their goals. Since forming Blanket Coverage, Richard Sherman and the Blanket Coverage team have made it their mission to provide school supplies for students across America. Richard has visited several elementary and high schools, speaking to the student body on making the world a better place than when they entered it."

www.richardsherman25.com/pages/foundation

Alex Smith

The Alex Smith Foundation: "The Alex Smith Foundation provides foster teens with the with tools and resources needed to transition to successful adulthood by developing and promoting Education, Advocacy, Mentoring, Housing, Internship and Jobs programs."

www.alexsmithfoundation.org

Torrey Smith

Torrey Smith Family Fund: "We work towards creating a society that is equitable and compassionate. To that end, our simple mission is to assist the communities in which we have been fortunate to live and work. Whether we are supporting, children, animals or adults, TSFF is determined to leave the world better than we found it."

www.torreysmith.org

Kenny Stills

The Kenny Stills Foundation: "The Kenny Stills Foundation is committed to empowering underserved communities, improving quality of life and creating opportunity through education and enriching experience."
www.kstills.com/kennystillsfoundation

The Still Growing Summit: "The Still Growing Summit is an organization funded by Kenny Stills built to spread awareness, and provide special resources to Underserved communities while helping kids and their families have an open dialogue about mental and emotional wellness."
www.stillgrowingsummit.com

Delanie Walker

The Delanie Walker Gives Back Foundation: "The Delanie Walker Gives Back Foundation was founded to provide inner-city and low-income children with the educational opportunities and resources to reach their full potential and beat the odds. The major community outreach programs of Delanie Walker Gives Back include Back to School COOL, free dental visits for low income children and an annual free football camp for kids 8-14 in Pomona."
www.delaniewalkeronline.com

Russell Wilson

Why Not You Foundation: "The Why Not You Foundation was launched in 2014 by Russell Wilson and is dedicated to creating real and lasting change in the world by motivating, empowering

and preparing today's youth to be tomorrow's leaders."
www.whynotyoufdn.org

Cam Newton
Cam Newton Foundation: "The Cam Newton Foundation is committed to enhancing the lives of young people by addressing their socioeconomic, educational, physical and emotional needs. The overarching CNF theme is 'Every 1 Matters.' Under that mantra, three focus areas exist: Every 1 Learns, Every 1 Plays, Every 1 Gives."
www.cam1newton.com

ACKNOWLEDGMENTS

This book is essentially four years in the making, and the idea for it started in 2016 when speaking with Colin Kaepernick at his locker, as he explained his reasons for protesting. I told him, "I'm going to write a book on all of this one day; you guys are heroes." His response: "Just be fair." Those brief interviews appear here.

If there's one thing I want people to know about Kaepernick, it is that he is a genuinely good person, honorable, and dedicated to his cause. My guess is he will spend the rest of his life dedicated to improving—and protecting—the lives of black and brown people. He is a noble man fighting for a noble cause.

My overall thank you goes to the player protesters (and their supporters). These are extremely brave people who risked not just their careers but also the wrath of a vindictive POTUS and a right-wing media ecosystem determined to intimidate, humiliate, and undercut the movement.

I also want to thank Nessa Diab, one of the smartest and kindest people I've ever known. If Kaepernick and Eric Reid are the fathers of the movement, she is its mother.

My interviews with Reid happened in San Francisco, later when he was with the Carolina Panthers (also while at his locker), and once over the telephone. Reid's integrity and fearlessness, combined with his loyalty to Kaepernick, are among some of the more impressive things about him.

Kenny Stills was thoughtful, smart, and kind with his time. I can't thank him enough.

Also, I wanted to thank three other people specifically in Richard Sherman, Martellus Bennett, and Michael Bennett. They are, and have been, some of the NFL's greatest truth tellers and honorable men.

I need to also thank the NFL coaches, players, team, and league officials who helped me who are not named in the book.

I also want to thank Sports Publishing and my editor Jason Katzman, who is one of the most skilled editors that I've ever worked with.

Thank you also to my agent, Andrew Stuart, from the Stuart Agency, who always tirelessly fights for his writers.

This is, in many ways, frightening times. What helps is clarity and an examination of how we got here. Hopefully this book illuminates an important part of recent American history.

ABOUT THE AUTHOR

Mike Freeman is a veteran sports journalist with more than 25 years of experience. Currently a sports business reporter for *Sportico*, he has covered the NFL for the *Dallas Morning News*, *Boston Globe*, *Washington Post*, *New York Times*, *Bleacher Report*, and CBS Sports. com. In addition, he has been a contributor to CNN, *The Jim Rome Show*, and *The Tony Kornheiser Show*. Freeman is the author of eight books, including *Jim Brown: The Fierce Life of an American Hero* and *Snake: The Legendary Life of Ken Stabler*.

SOURCES

Abdul-Jabbar, Kareem. "Insulting Colin Kaepernick Says More About Our Patriotism Than His," *Washington Post*, August 30, 2016.

Agiesta, Jennifer. "CNN poll: Americans split on anthem protests," CNN, September 30, 2017.

Associated Press. "NFL Antitrust Testimony Steered in Different Direction," *Los Angeles Times*, July 9, 1992.

Ax, Joseph. "Presidential Hopeful Booker Vows to End 'Moral Vandalism' of Trump Immigration Policy," *Reuters*, July 2, 2019.

Babb, Kent. "NFC Championship: 49ers Storm Back to Beat Falcons 28-24, Win Super Bowl Berth," *Washington Post*, January 20, 2013.

Babb, Kent. "The making of Colin Kaepernick," *Washington Post*, September 7, 2017.

Beaton, Andrew. "Colin Kaepernick's Glaring Absence at the Super Bowl," *Wall Street Journal*, February 1, 2020.

Bell, Gregg. "Seahawks' Wilson Speaks Out About Protests, Makes Sherman Proud." Herald*Net*, September 28, 2017.

Berkow, Ira. "The Case of Hodges vs. the N.B.A." *New York Times*, December 25, 1996.

Black, Eric. "Sen. Graham Would Benefit Greatly From an Orwellian 'Memory Hole,'" *MinnPost*, December 11, 2019.

Blaskey, Sarah. "Trump Says Americans Should 'Stand Proudly' for the Anthem. Video Shows Him Pointing, Fidgeting at Super Bowl Party," *Miami Herald*, February 4, 2020.

Bonesteel, Matt. "'We Can't Have the Inmates Running the Prison': Anti-Protest NFL Owners Are Fighting a Losing Battle," *Washington Post*, October 28, 2017.

Branch, John. "The Awakening of Colin Kaepernick," *New York Times*, September 7, 2017.

Bryant, Howard. *The Heritage: Black Athletes, a Divided America, and the Politics of Patriotism.* Beacon Press (Boston), 2018.

Breech, John. "Colin Kaepernick Disputes Report He Fought Aldon Smith Before Arrest," CBS Sports, August 8, 2015.

Brinson, Will. "Chip Kelly Says Colin Kaepernick Was Never a Distraction, Will Be Better in 2017," CBS Sports, June 29, 2017.

Brown, Duane, and Eric Reid. "Race, Policing and the Voice of the NFL Player." *Sports Illustrated*, July 15, 2016.

Bushnell, Henry. "Why Eric Reid Knelt, and Why His Protest is 'Not Gonna Be Shut Down,'" Yahoo! Sports, October 5, 2018.

By the Dawn's Early Light: Chris Jackson's Journey to Islam. Directed by Zareena Grewal. 2004; New York, NY: Cinema Guild.

Carroll, Scott. "Former U.S. Army Gen. Wesley Clark Says Colin Kaepernick, Nike on 'Right Side of History,'" KATV, September 6, 2018.

CBS News. "About Two Dozen Players Kneel for National Anthem in London," CBS News, September 24, 2017.

Chan, Melissa. "Read LeBron James and Carmelo Anthony's Powerful Speech on Race at the ESPY Awards." *Time*, July 14, 2016.

Chasmar, Jessica. "Lindsey Graham Rips Colin Kaepernick for Iran Criticism: 'He's a Loser On and Off the Field,'" *Washington Times*, January 6, 2020.

Clark, Dartunorro. "Democrat Beto O'Rourke, in Viral Video, Defends NFL Protests." NBC News, August 24, 2018.

Clark, Liz. "Eric Reid Won't Say if He'll Protest During Anthem, but Case Versus NFL Will Continue," *Washington Post*, October 2, 2018.

Cobb, James C. "When Martin Luther King Jr. Was Killed, He Was Less Popular Than Donald Trump Is Today," *USA Today*, April 4, 2018.

Crnogaj, Murray. "History of NBA Activism: Hodges Urges Magic and Jordan to Boycott Game 1 of the 1991 NBA Finals," Basketball Network, June 5, 2020.

Daniels, Tim. "Colin Kaepernick Accepts Blame for 49ers' Super Bowl Loss to Ravens," *Bleacher Report*, February 5, 2013.

Diaz, Daniella. "Obama defends Kaepernick's anthem protest." CNN, September 29, 2016.

Duprese, Olivia. "Analysis: How the Right and Left-Wing Media Have Covered the Kaepernick Scandal," MediaFile, September 8, 2016.

Durkee, Travis. "'Great White Heroes' Tom Brady, Peyton Manning Should Join Colin Kaepernick's Cause, Former Player Says," *Sporting News*, June 1, 2019.

Elving, Ron. "With Latest Nativist Rhetoric, Trump Takes America Back to Where It Came From." NPR, July 16, 2019.

Feinberg, Ayal, Regina Branton, and Valerie Martinez-Ebers, "Counties That Hosted a 2016 Trump Rally Saw a 226 percent Increase in Hate Crimes," *Washington Post*, March 23, 2019.

Florio, Mike. "Donald Trump Calls Out Colin Kaepernick, Again." NBC Sports, March 20, 2017.

Florio, Mike. "Kneeling Issue Arises During Bengals' Meeting with Eric Reid," NBC Sports, April 11, 2018.

Freedman, Samuel G. *Breaking the Line: The Season in Black College Football That Transformed the Sport and Changed the Course of Civil Rights*, Simon & Schuster (New York), 2013.

Freeman, Michael. *Two Minute Warning: How Concussions, Crime, and Controversy Could Kill the NFL (And What the League Could Do To Survive)*, Triumph Books (Chicago), 2015.

Freeman, Mike. "Colin Kaepernick Sentenced to NFL Limbo for the Crime of Speaking His Mind." *Bleacher Report*, March 18, 2017.

Freeman, Mike. "Beyond the Anthem: Inside NFL Locker Rooms on Trump, Kap, Charlottesville & Race." *Bleacher Report*, September 8, 2017.

Garcia-Navarro, Lulu. "'Heroic, But He's No Hero': Revisiting Football Great Jim Brown," NPR, May 13, 2018.

Gaydos, Ryan. "Hockey Coach Who Went Viral for Pro-National Anthem Message: 'I Take Pride in My Country'," Fox News, July 11, 2019.

Goldberg, Rob. "Jim Brown on Donald Trump: 'I Find Myself Really Pulling for the President'," *Bleacher Report*, August 22, 2018.

Grenoble, Ryan. "Bar With Homemade 'Lynch Kaepernick' Doormat Can't Figure Out Why Everyone Is Calling It Racist," *Huffington Post*, September 28, 2017.

Halberstam, David. *Playing for Keeps: Michael Jordan and the World He Made*, Random House (New York), 1999.

Hannity, Sean. "Just Don't Do It," Fox News, September 5, 2018.

Helsel, Phil. "Ex-CIA Director Brennan Defends NFL Protests, Says Trump Should Focus on Puerto Rico." NBC News, October 1, 2017.

Hill, Jemele. "Beto O'Rourke Grabbed a Political Third Rail—And Electrified His Campaign." *The Atlantic*, October 27, 2018.

Hirschfeld Davis, Julie, and Michael D. Shear. *Border Wars: Inside Trump's Assault on Immigration*, Simon & Schuster (New York), 2019.

Hogg, Dave. "The Military Paid Pro Sports Teams $10.4 Million for Patriotic Displays, Troop Tributes," *SBNation*, November 4, 2015.

Hruby, Patrick. "Three years in the NFL wilderness: what Colin Kaepernick lost – and won," *The Guardian*, August 19, 2019.

Inman, Cam. "Colin Kaepernick Again Defends Relationship with Aldon Smith, Chastises Internet Trolls," *Mercury News*, August 12, 2015.

Jenkins, Sally. "Colin Kaepernick Reminds Us That Dissent is a Form of Patriotism Too," *Washington Post*, September 8, 2016.

Kenny Stills. Directed by Lukas Korver. 2018; Los Angeles, CA: Park Stories.

Kilgore, Adam. "For Decades, the NFL Wrapped Itself in the Flag. Now, That's Made Business Uneasy," *Washington Post*, September 7, 2018.

Kimes, Mina. "The Search For Aaron Rodgers," ESPN, August 30, 2017.

King, Alexandra. "Warriors Coach Steve Kerr on Why Team Still Won't be Visiting the White House." CNN, November 26, 2017.

Klar, Rebecca. "Minnesota 'Teacher of the Year' Kneels During College Football Championship," *The Hill*, January 1, 2020.

Korver, Kyle. "Privileged," *Players' Tribune*, April 8, 2019.

Kurtz, Jason. "Trump's 'SOB' Remark Moves NFL Player to Kneel During Anthem." CNN, December 22, 2017.

Lee, Esther. "Colin Kaepernick Details Racial Struggle From His Childhood," *US Weekly*, October 8, 2015.

Lipsyte, Robert. "Donald Trump's War on Black Athletes." *The Nation*, July 12, 2018.

Lopez, Andrew. "Former LSU Safety Eric Reid Unafraid to Sacrifice NFL Career for his Principles." NOLA.com, *Times-Picayune*, March 13, 2018.

MacCambridge, Michael. *America's Game: The Epic Story of How Pro Football Captured a Nation*, Random House (New York), 2004.

Maese, Rick. "Mahmoud Abdul-Rauf on Kaepernick Controversy: 'It's a Duplicate Pretty Much'," *Washington Post*, August 24, 2017.

Maiocco, Matt. "Kaepernick, Tomsula Disappointed; Do 49ers Make Changes?" NBC Sports, October 22, 2015.

Maloney, Jack. "Sefolosha to Donate Large Portion of $4M Settlement from Police Brutality Lawsuit," CBS Sports, April 7, 2017.

Manfred, Tony. "The Cancer-Stricken Coach of The Indianapolis Colts Gave One of the Most Inspirational Postgame Speeches You'll Ever See," *Business Insider*, November 6, 2012.

Marshall, Serena and Jim Avila. "NFL Admits More Than $700K in Taxpayer Funds May Have Been Used for Military Tributes," ABC News, May 20, 2016.

Martin, Michel. "The Veteran and NFL Player Who Advised Kaepernick to Take A Knee," NPR, September 9, 2018.

Mihoces, Gary. "Colin Kaepernick, 49ers Thrash Packers 45-31," *USA Today*, January 12, 2013.

Moore, Sam. "Rihanna on Turning Down the Super Bowl Halftime Show: 'I Just Couldn't Be a Sellout'," NME, October 9, 2019.

Morin, Rebecca. "Trump Says Pence's Trip to NFL Game Was 'Long Planned'," *Politico*, October 9, 2017.

"Negro Star of the Chicago Eleven Thrills 18,000 by Dazzling Runs as Cardinals Down Boston," *Boston Globe*, October 17, 1932.

Novy-Williams, Eben and Scott Soshnick. "XFL Players Who Kneel During the Anthem Will Face 'Consequences'," *Bloomberg*, February 7, 2020.

Oriard, Michael. *Brand NFL: Making and Selling America's Favorite Sport*, University of North Carolina Press (Chapel Hill), 2007.

Patterson, Chip. "Jim Harbaugh Praises Colin Kaepernick, Compares Efforts to Muhammad Ali and Jackie Robinson," CBS Sports, June 23, 2020.

Pearlman, Jeff. *Football for a Buck: The Crazy Rise and Crazier Demise of the USFL.* Houghton Mifflin Harcourt (New York), 2018.

Pergament, Alan. "Showtime Documentary on Racism Highlights Former Bills Marlin Briscoe, James Harris," *Buffalo News*, August 8, 2013.

Peter, Josh. "Colin Kaepernick: I'm not anti-American, will donate $1 million," *USA Today*, September 1, 2016.

Pitofsky, Marina. "GOP Rep Releases Campaign Ad Ripping Kaepernick, 'The Squad'," *The Hill*, January 7, 2020.

Polacek, Scott. "Bill Polian Says Lamar Jackson Is 'Short,' Should Move to WR in the NFL," *Bleacher Report*, February 20, 2018.

Polacek, Scott. "Antonio Cromartie Believes Colts Cut Him for Kneeling." *Bleacher Report*, October 31, 2019.

Real Sports with Bryant Gumbel. HBO, September 27, 2017.

"The Reintegration of the NFL." NFL Ops, n.d.

Rhoden, William C. *Third and a Mile: From Fritz Pollard to Michael Vick—An Oral History of the Trials, Tears and Triumphs of the Black Quarterback*, ESPN Books (New York), 2007.

Rosman, Katherine. "Jay-Z Takes on the Super Bowl," *New York Times*, February 1, 2020.

Salaam, Khalid. "Colin Kaepernick's Legacy Might Look a Lot Like Mahmoud Abdul-Rauf's," *Bleacher Report*, September 9, 2016.

Salazar, Sebastian. "USWNT's Megan Rapinoe Kneels During National Anthem in Solidarity with Colin Kaepernick," NBC Sports, September 4, 2016.

Schefter, Adam. "Seahawks Postpone Visit After Colin Kaepernick Won't Say If He'll Stop Kneeling During Anthem," ESPN, April 13, 2018.

Schoenfeld, Bruce. "The Justice League," *Esquire*, September 25, 2017.

Scott, Eugene. "Trump's Most Insulting—and Violent—Language is Often Reserved for Immigrants." *Washington Post*, October 3, 2019.

Shea, Rich. "Paul Robeson Football Star," *Rutgers Today*, March 13, 2019.

Sherman, Gabriel. "The Season from Hell: Inside Roger Goodell's Ruthless Football Machine," *GQ*, January 20, 2015.

Shut Up and Dribble. Directed by Gotham Chopra. 2018; Showtime Sports et al.

Smith, Michael David. "Trump to NFL Owners: Fire Players Who Don't Stand for the National Anthem." NBC Sports, September 22, 2017.

Smith, Thomas G. "Outside the Pale: The Exclusion of Blacks from the National Football League, 1934–1946," *Journal of Sport History* 15, no. 3 (Winter, 1988): 255–281.

Spain, Kevin. "HBO's Bryant Gumbel Thanks Trump for Energizing Modern American Athlete," *USA Today*, September 26, 2017.

Spears, Marc J. "Abdul-Rauf: Kaepernick's Situation 'Mirrors What I Went Through'," *The Undefeated*, June 25, 2017.

Sports Illustrated. "How Far Have We Come?" *Sports Illustrated*, August 5, 1991.

Sports Illustrated. "Race, Policing and the Voice of the NFL Player," *Sports Illustrated*, July 15, 2016.

Squadron, Alex. "Former Chicago Bull Craig Hodges Tells His Story, Opens Up About NBA Activism," *Slam*, April 11, 2019.

Stelter, Brian, and Chris Isidore. "Trump Attacks ESPN After Anchor Calls him a White Supremacist." CNN, September 15, 2017.

Tribune Political Team. "Political Cornflakes: The grudge-holding abilities of President Trump are on full display with passing of Sen. McCain," *Salt Lake Tribune*, August 27, 2018.

Veeck, Bill, with Ed Lynn, *Veeck—As in Wreck: The Autobiography of Bill Veeck*. Putnam (New York), 1962.

Veterans for Kaepernick. "An Open Letter of Support for Colin Kaepernick From American Military Veterans," *Medium*, September 3, 2016.

Voth, Bill. "With Deep Military Ties, Eric Reid's Family Supports His Cause," Carolina Pathers, November 3, 2018.

Wagoner, Nick. "Transcript of Colin Kaepernick's Comments About Sitting During National Anthem," ESPN, August 29, 2016.

Wagoner, Nick. "Colin Kaepernick: 'I'll Continue to Sit'," ABC News, August 30, 2016.

Wamsley, Laurel, and Bobby Allyn. "Neo-Nazi Who Killed Charlottesville Protester Is Sentenced to Life in Prison." NPR, June 28, 2019.

Washington, Jesse. "Still No Anthem, Still No Regrets for Mahmoud Abdul-Rauf," *The Undefeated*, September 1, 2016.

Watkins, Eli. "Pence Leaves Colts Game after Protest During Anthem," CNN, October 9, 2017.

Weiner, Natalie. "The NFL's Last Men Kneeling," *Bleacher Report*, January 4, 2018.

Wickersham, Seth. "Why Richard Sherman Can't Let Go of Seattle's Super Bowl Loss," *ESPN: The Magazine*, May 25, 2017.

Wilson, Aaron. "Houston Police Chief Art Acevedo Meets with Texans' Kenny Stills, Praises His Character, Ideas." *Houston Chronicle*, September 17, 2019.

Wulf, Steve. "All Hell Broke Loose," ABC News, January 21, 2014.

Yükse, Canberk. "US: Pennsylvania Fire Chief Resigns Over Racial Slur," Anadolu Agency, September 27, 2017.

Zaru, Deena. "Beyoncé Gets Political at Super Bowl, Pays Tribute to 'Black Lives Matter'," CNN, August 17, 2017.

Zirin, David. "'A Soulless Coward': Coach Gregg Popovich Responds to Trump." *The Nation*, October 16, 2017.

Zirin, David. "This Year's Super Bowl Was Blatantly Propagandistic," *The Nation*, February 4, 2020.